BRITISH ENG

ENGLISH CZECH

THEME-BASED DICTIONARY

Contains over 5000 commonly
used words

T&P BOOKS PUBLISHING

Theme-based dictionary British English-Czech - 5000 words
British English collection

By Andrey Taranov

T&P Books vocabularies are intended for helping you learn, memorize and review foreign words. The dictionary is divided into themes, covering all major spheres of everyday activities, business, science, culture, etc.

The process of learning words using T&P Books' theme-based dictionaries gives you the following advantages:

- Correctly grouped source information predetermines success at subsequent stages of word memorization
- Availability of words derived from the same root allowing memorization of word units (rather than separate words)
- Small units of words facilitate the process of establishing associative links needed for consolidation of vocabulary
- Level of language knowledge can be estimated by the number of learned words

T&P Books Publishing
www.tpbooks.com

ISBN: 978-1-78400-188-9

This book is also available in E-book formats.
Please visit www.tpbooks.com or the major online bookstores.

CZECH THEME-BASED DICTIONARY
British English collection

T&P Books vocabularies are intended to help you learn, memorize, and review foreign words. The vocabulary contains over 5000 commonly used words arranged thematically.

- Vocabulary contains the most commonly used words
- Recommended as an addition to any language course
- Meets the needs of beginners and advanced learners of foreign languages
- Convenient for daily use, revision sessions, and self-testing activities
- Allows you to assess your vocabulary

Special features of the vocabulary

- Words are organized according to their meaning, not alphabetically
- Words are presented in three columns to facilitate the reviewing and self-testing processes
- Words in groups are divided into small blocks to facilitate the learning process
- The vocabulary offers a convenient and simple transcription of each foreign word

The vocabulary has 155 topics including:

Basic Concepts, Numbers, Colors, Months, Seasons, Units of Measurement, Clothing & Accessories, Food & Nutrition, Restaurant, Family Members, Relatives, Character, Feelings, Emotions, Diseases, City, Town, Sightseeing, Shopping, Money, House, Home, Office, Working in the Office, Import & Export, Marketing, Job Search, Sports, Education, Computer, Internet, Tools, Nature, Countries, Nationalities and more …

TABLE OF CONTENTS

PRONUNCIATION GUIDE

Letter	Czech example	T&P phonetics alphabet	English example

Vowels

A a	pas	[a]	shorter than in ask
Á á	pás	[aː]	calf, palm
E e	let	[ɛ]	man, bad
É é	létat	[ɛː]	longer than bed, fell
Ě ě	dělat	[e]	elm, medal
I i	platit	[ɪ]	big, America
Í í	peníze	[iː]	feet, meter
O o	ovoce	[o]	pod, John
Ó ó	sezóna	[oː]	fall, bomb
U u	kupovat	[u]	book
Ú ú	úroda	[uː]	pool, room
Ů ů	stůl	[uː]	pool, room
Y y	byt	[ɪ]	big, America
Ý ý	velký	[iː]	feet, meter

Consonants

B b	budova	[b]	baby, book
C c	cesta	[ts]	cats, tsetse fly
Č č	čas	[ʧ]	church, French
D d	dole	[d]	day, doctor
Ď ď	d'ábel	[dʲ]	median, radio
F f	fronta	[f]	face, food
G g	generace	[g]	game, gold
H h	hora	[ɦ]	huge, humor
J j	jméno	[j]	yes, New York
K k	kytara	[k]	clock, kiss
L l	lidé	[l]	lace, people
M m	majitel	[m]	magic, milk
N n	nájem	[n]	name, normal
Ň ň	daň	[ɲ]	canyon, new
P p	pokuta	[p]	pencil, private
R r	rada	[r]	rice, radio
Ř ř	řada	[rʒ]	forge
S s	sako	[s]	city, boss
Š š	šaty	[ʃ]	machine, shark
T t	taška	[t]	tourist, trip

Letter	Czech example	T&P phonetics alphabet	English example
Ť ť	pleť	[t]	tune, student
V v	vlasy	[v]	very, river
Z z	mozek	[z]	zebra, please
Ž ž	život	[ʒ]	forge, pleasure

Combinations of letters

ch	chlapec	[h]	huge, hat
au	auto	[au]	loud, powder
eu	euro	[ɛu]	Congo, koala
ou ˙	koupit	[ou]	know, hope

Comments

˙ Standard Czech and, with a few minor exceptions, all of the Czech dialects have fixed initial stress.

ABBREVIATIONS
used in the dictionary

ab.	-	about
adj	-	adjective
adv	-	adverb
anim.	-	animate
as adj	-	attributive noun used as adjective
e.g.	-	for example
etc.	-	et cetera
fam.	-	familiar
fem.	-	feminine
form.	-	formal
inanim.	-	inanimate
masc.	-	masculine
math	-	mathematics
mil.	-	military
n	-	noun
pl	-	plural
pron.	-	pronoun
sb	-	somebody
sing.	-	singular
sth	-	something
v aux	-	auxiliary verb
vi	-	intransitive verb
vi, vt	-	intransitive, transitive verb
vt	-	transitive verb

m	-	masculine noun
f	-	feminine noun
m pl	-	masculine plural
f pl	-	feminine plural
n pl	-	neuter plural
m, f	-	masculine, feminine

BASIC CONCEPTS

Basic concepts. Part 1

1. Pronouns

I, me	já	[ja:]
you	ty	[tɪ]
he	on	[on]
she	ona	[ona]
we	my	[mɪ]
you (to a group)	vy	[vɪ]
they (inanim.)	ony	[onɪ]
they (anim.)	oni	[oni]

2. Greetings. Salutations. Farewells

Hello! (fam.)	Dobrý den!	[dobrɪ: dɛn]
Hello! (form.)	Dobrý den!	[dobrɪ: dɛn]
Good morning!	Dobré jitro!	[dobrɛ: jɪtro]
Good afternoon!	Dobrý den!	[dobrɪ: dɛn]
Good evening!	Dobrý večer!	[dobrɪ: vɛtʃer]
to say hello	zdravit	[zdrawit]
Hi! (hello)	Ahoj!	[agoj]
greeting (n)	pozdrav (m)	[pozdrav]
to greet (vt)	zdravit	[zdrawit]
How are you?	Jak se máte?	[jak sɛ ma:tɛ]
What's new?	Co je nového?	[tso je novɛ:go]
Bye-Bye! Goodbye!	Na shledanou!	[na sɦlɛdanou]
See you soon!	Brzy na shledanou!	[brzɪ na sɦlɛdanou]
Farewell!	Sbohem!	[zbogɛm]
to say goodbye	loučit se	[loutʃit sɛ]
Cheers!	Ahoj!	[agoj]
Thank you! Cheers!	Děkuji!	[dekujɪ]
Thank you very much!	Děkuji mnohokrát!	[dekujɪ mnogokra:t]
My pleasure!	Prosím	[prosi:m]
Don't mention it!	Nemoci se dočkat	[nɛmotsi sɛ dotʃkat]
It was nothing	Není zač	[nɛni: zatʃ]
Excuse me! (fam.)	Promiň!	[promiɲ]
Excuse me! (form.)	Promiňte!	[promiɲtɛ]
to excuse (forgive)	omlouvat	[omlouvat]

to apologize (vi)	omlouvat se	[omlouvat sɛ]
My apologies	Má soustrast	[ma: soustrast]
I'm sorry!	Promiňte!	[promiɲtɛ]
to forgive (vt)	omlouvat	[omlouvat]
please (adv)	prosím	[prosi:m]

Don't forget!	Nezapomeňte!	[nɛzapomɛɲtɛ]
Certainly!	Jistě!	[jıste]
Of course not!	Rozhodně ne!	[rozgodne nɛ]
Okay! (I agree)	Souhlasím!	[souglasi:m]
That's enough!	Dost!	[dost]

3. How to address

mister, sir	Pane	[panɛ]
madam	Paní	[pani:]
miss	Slečno	[slɛtʃno]
young man	Mladý muži	[mladı: muʒi]
young man (little boy)	Chlapče	[ɦlaptʃe]
miss (little girl)	Děvče	[devtʃe]

4. Cardinal numbers. Part 1

0 zero	nula (f)	[nula]
1 one	jeden	[jedɛn]
2 two	dva	[dva]
3 three	tři	[trʃi]
4 four	čtyři	[tʃtırʒi]

5 five	pět	[pʰet]
6 six	šest	[ʃɛst]
7 seven	sedm	[sɛdm]
8 eight	osm	[osm]
9 nine	devět	[dɛvʰet]

10 ten	deset	[dɛsɛt]
11 eleven	jedenáct	[jedɛna:tst]
12 twelve	dvanáct	[dvana:tst]
13 thirteen	třináct	[trʃina:tst]
14 fourteen	čtrnáct	[tʃtrna:tst]

15 fifteen	patnáct	[patna:tst]
16 sixteen	šestnáct	[ʃɛstna:tst]
17 seventeen	sedmnáct	[sɛdmna:tst]
18 eighteen	osmnáct	[osmna:tst]
19 nineteen	devatenáct	[dɛvatɛna:tst]

20 twenty	dvacet	[dvatset]
21 twenty-one	jedenadvacet	[jedɛnadvatset]
22 twenty-two	dvaadvacet	[dva:dvatset]
23 twenty-three	třiadvacet	[trʃiadvatset]
30 thirty	třicet	[trʃitset]

31 thirty-one	jedenatřicet	[jedɛnatrʃitset]
32 thirty-two	dvaatřicet	[dva:trʃitset]
33 thirty-three	třiatřicet	[trʃiatrʃitset]

40 forty	čtyřicet	[ʧtɪrʒitset]
41 forty-one	jedenačtyřicet	[jedɛnaʧtɪrʒitset]
42 forty-two	dvaačtyřicet	[dva:ʧtɪrʒitset]
43 forty-three	třiačtyřicet	[trʃiaʧtɪrʒitset]

50 fifty	padesát	[padesa:t]
51 fifty-one	jedenapadesát	[jedɛnapadɛsa:t]
52 fifty-two	dvaapadesát	[dva:padɛsa:t]
53 fifty-three	třiapadesát	[trʃiapadɛsa:t]

60 sixty	šedesát	[ʃedɛsa:t]
61 sixty-one	jedenašedesát	[jedɛnaʃedɛsa:t]
62 sixty-two	dvaašedesát	[dva:ʃedɛsa:t]
63 sixty-three	třiašedesát	[trʃiaʃedɛsa:t]

70 seventy	sedmdesát	[sɛdmdɛsa:t]
71 seventy-one	jedenasedmdesát	[jedɛnasɛdmdɛsa:t]
72 seventy-two	dvaasedmdesát	[dva:sɛdmdɛsa:t]
73 seventy-three	třiasedmdesát	[trʃiasɛdmdɛsa:t]

80 eighty	osmdesát	[osmdɛsa:t]
81 eighty-one	jedenaosmdesát	[jedɛnaosmdɛsa:t]
82 eighty-two	dvaaosmdesát	[dva:osmdɛsa:t]
83 eighty-three	třiaosmdesát	[trʃiaosmdɛsa:t]

90 ninety	devadesát	[dɛvadesa:t]
91 ninety-one	jedenadevadesát	[jedɛnadɛvadɛsa:t]
92 ninety-two	dvaadevadesát	[dva:dɛvadɛsa:t]
93 ninety-three	třiadevadesát	[trʃiadɛvadɛsa:t]

5. Cardinal numbers. Part 2

100 one hundred	sto	[sto]
200 two hundred	dvě stě	[dvʰe ste]
300 three hundred	tři sta	[trʃi sta]
400 four hundred	čtyři sta	[ʧtɪrʒi sta]
500 five hundred	pět set	[pʰet sɛt]

600 six hundred	šest set	[ʃest sɛt]
700 seven hundred	sedm set	[sɛdm sɛt]
800 eight hundred	osm set	[osm sɛt]
900 nine hundred	devět set	[dɛvʰet sɛt]

1000 one thousand	tisíc (m)	[tisi:ʦ]
2000 two thousand	dva tisíce	[dva tisi:ʦe]
3000 three thousand	tři tisíce	[trʃi tisi:ʦe]
10000 ten thousand	deset tisíc	[dɛsɛt tisi:ʦ]
one hundred thousand	sto tisíc	[sto tisi:ʦ]
million	milión (m)	[milijo:n]
billion	miliarda (f)	[milijarda]

6. Ordinal numbers

first (adj)	první	[prvni:]
second (adj)	druhý	[drugɪ:]
third (adj)	třetí	[trʃɛti:]
fourth (adj)	čtvrtý	[ʧtvrtɪ:]
fifth (adj)	pátý	[pa:tɪ:]
sixth (adj)	šestý	[ʃɛstɪ:]
seventh (adj)	sedmý	[sɛdmɪ:]
eighth (adj)	osmý	[osmɪ:]
ninth (adj)	devátý	[dɛva:tɪ:]
tenth (adj)	desátý	[dɛsa:tɪ:]

7. Numbers. Fractions

fraction	zlomek (m)	[zlomɛk]
one half	polovina (f)	[polowina]
one third	třetina (f)	[trʃɛtina]
one quarter	čtvrtina (f)	[ʧtvrtina]
one eighth	osmina (f)	[osmina]
one tenth	desetina (f)	[dɛsɛtina]
two thirds	dvě třetiny (f)	[dvʰe trʃɛtinɪ]
three quarters	tři čtvrtiny (f)	[trʃi ʧtvrtinɪ]

8. Numbers. Basic operations

subtraction	odčítání (n)	[odʧi:ta:ni:]
to subtract (vi, vt)	odčítat	[odʧi:tat]
division	dělení (n)	[delɛni:]
to divide (vt)	dělit	[delit]
addition	sčítání (n)	[sʧi:ta:ni:]
to add up (vt)	sečíst	[sɛʧi:st]
to add (vi)	přidávat	[prʃida:vat]
multiplication	násobení (n)	[na:sobɛni:]
to multiply (vt)	násobit	[na:sobit]

9. Numbers. Miscellaneous

digit, figure	číslice (f)	[ʧi:slitse]
number	číslo (n)	[ʧi:slo]
numeral	číslovka (f)	[ʧi:slovka]
minus	minus (m)	[mi:nus]
plus	plus (m)	[plus]
formula	vzorec (m)	[vzorɛts]
calculation	vypočítávání (n)	[vɪpoʧi:ta:va:ni:]
to count (vt)	počítat	[poʧi:tat]

| to count up | vypočítávat | [vɪpotʃiːtaːvat] |
| to compare (vt) | srovnávat | [srovnaːvat] |

How much? How many?	Kolik?	[kolik]
sum, total	součet (m)	[soutʃet]
result	výsledek (m)	[vɪːslɛdɛk]
remainder	zůstatek (m)	[zuːstatɛk]

a few ...	několik	[nekolik]
few, little (adv)	trochu ...	[troɦu]
the rest	zbytek (m)	[zbɪtɛk]
one and a half	půl druhého	[puːl drugɛːgo]
dozen	tucet (m)	[tutset]

in half (adv)	napolovic	[napolowits]
equally (evenly)	stejně	[stɛjne]
half	polovina (f)	[polowina]
time (instance)	krát	[kraːt]

10. The most important verbs. Part 1

to advise (vt)	radit	[radit]
to agree (say yes)	souhlasit	[souglasit]
to answer (vi, vt)	odpovídat	[odpowiːdat]

to apologize (vi)	omlouvat se	[omlouvat sɛ]
to arrive (vi)	přijíždět	[prʃijɪːʒdet]
to ask (~ oneself)	ptát se	[ptaːt sɛ]
to ask (~ sb to do sth)	prosit	[prosit]

to be (vi)	být	[bɪːt]
to be afraid	bát se	[baːt sɛ]
to be hungry	mít hlad	[miːt glad]
to be interested in ...	zajímat se	[zajɪːmat sɛ]
to be needed	být potřebný	[bɪːt potrʃɛbnɪː]
to be surprised	divit se	[diwit sɛ]
to be thirsty	mít žízeň	[miːt ʒiːzɛɲ]

to begin (vt)	začínat	[zatʃiːnat]
to belong to ...	patřit	[patrʃit]
to boast (vi)	vychloubat se	[vɪɦloubat sɛ]
to break (split into pieces)	lámat	[laːmat]

to call (for help)	volat	[volat]
can (v aux)	moci	[motsi]
to catch (vt)	chytat	[ɦɪtat]
to change (vt)	změnit	[zmnenit]
to choose (select)	vybírat	[vɪbiːrat]

to come down	jít dolů	[jɪːt dolu]
to come in (enter)	vcházet	[vɦaːzet]
to compare (vt)	porovnávat	[porovnaːvat]
to complain (vi, vt)	stěžovat si	[steʒovat si]
to confuse (mix up)	plést	[plɛːst]

to continue (vt)	pokračovat	[pokratʃovat]
to control (vt)	kontrolovat	[kontrolovat]
to cook (dinner)	vařit	[varʒit]
to cost (vt)	stát	[staːt]

to count (add up)	počítat	[potʃiːtat]
to count on …	spoléhat na …	[spolɛːgat na]
to create (vt)	vytvořit	[vɪtvorʒit]
to cry (weep)	plakat	[plakat]

11. The most important verbs. Part 2

to deceive (vi, vt)	podvádět	[podvaːdet]
to decorate (tree, street)	zdobit	[zdobit]
to defend (a country, etc.)	bránit	[braːnit]
to demand (request firmly)	žádat	[ʒaːdat]

to dig (vt)	rýt	[rɪːt]
to discuss (vt)	projednávat	[projednaːvat]
to do (vt)	dělat	[delat]
to doubt (have doubts)	pochybovat	[pofɪbovat]
to drop (let fall)	pouštět	[pouʃtet]

to exist (vi)	existovat	[ɛgzistovat]
to expect (foresee)	předvídat	[prʃɛdwiːdat]
to explain (vt)	vysvětlovat	[vɪsvʰetlovat]

to fall (vi)	padat	[padat]
to fancy (vt)	líbit se	[liːbit sɛ]
to find (vt)	nacházet	[nafaːzɛt]
to finish (vt)	končit	[kontʃit]
to fly (vi)	letět	[lɛtet]
to follow … (come after)	následovat	[naːslɛdovat]
to forget (vi, vt)	zapomínat	[zapomiːnat]
to forgive (vt)	odpouštět	[odpouʃtet]

to give (vt)	dávat	[daːvat]
to give a hint	narážet	[naraːʒet]
to go (on foot)	jít	[jɪːt]
to go for a swim	koupat se	[koupat sɛ]
to go out (from …)	vycházet	[vɪfaːzɛt]
to guess right	rozluštit	[rozluʃtit]

to have (vt)	mít	[miːt]
to have breakfast	snídat	[sniːdat]
to have dinner	večeřet	[vɛtʃerʒet]
to have lunch	obědvat	[obʰedvat]

to hear (vt)	slyšet	[slɪʃɛt]
to help (vt)	pomáhat	[pomaːgat]
to hide (vt)	schovávat	[sɦovaːvat]
to hope (vi, vt)	doufat	[doufat]
to hunt (vi, vt)	lovit	[lowit]
to hurry (vi)	spěchat	[spʰefat]

12. The most important verbs. Part 3

to inform (vt)	informovat	[informovat]
to insist (vi, vt)	trvat	[trvat]
to insult (vt)	urážet	[uraːʒet]
to invite (vt)	zvát	[zvaːt]
to joke (vi)	žertovat	[ʒertovat]
to keep (vt)	zachovávat	[zaɦovaːvat]
to keep silent	mlčet	[mltʃet]
to kill (vt)	zabíjet	[zabiːjet]
to know (sb)	znát	[znaːt]
to know (sth)	vědět	[vʰedet]
to laugh (vi)	smát se	[smaːt sɛ]
to liberate (city, etc.)	osvobozovat	[osvobozovat]
to look for … (search)	hledat	[glɛdat]
to love (sb)	milovat	[milovat]
to make a mistake	mýlit se	[mɪːlit sɛ]
to manage, to run	řídit	[rʒiːdit]
to mean (signify)	znamenat	[znamɛnat]
to mention (talk about)	zmiňovat se	[zminɔvat sɛ]
to miss (school, etc.)	zameškávat	[zameʃkaːvat]
to notice (see)	všímat si	[vʃiːmat si]
to object (vi, vt)	namítat	[namiːtat]
to observe (see)	pozorovat	[pozorovat]
to open (vt)	otvírat	[otwiːrat]
to order (meal, etc.)	objednávat	[obʰednaːvat]
to order (mil.)	rozkazovat	[rozkazovat]
to own (possess)	vlastnit	[vlastnit]
to participate (vi)	zúčastnit se	[zuːtʃastnit sɛ]
to pay (vi, vt)	platit	[platit]
to permit (vt)	dovolovat	[dovolovat]
to plan (vt)	plánovat	[plaːnovat]
to play (children)	hrát	[graːt]
to pray (vi, vt)	modlit se	[modlit sɛ]
to prefer (vt)	dávat přednost	[daːvat prʃɛdnost]
to promise (vt)	slibovat	[slibovat]
to pronounce (vt)	vyslovovat	[vɪslovovat]
to propose (vt)	nabízet	[nabiːzɛt]
to punish (vt)	trestat	[trɛstat]
to read (vi, vt)	číst	[tʃiːst]
to recommend (vt)	doporučovat	[doporutʃovat]
to refuse (vi, vt)	odmítat	[odmiːtat]
to regret (be sorry)	litovat	[litovat]
to rent (sth from sb)	pronajímat si	[pronajɪːmat si]
to repeat (say again)	opakovat	[opakovat]
to reserve, to book	rezervovat	[rɛzɛrvovat]
to run (vi)	běžet	[bʰeʒet]

13. The most important verbs. Part 4

to save (rescue)	zachraňovat	[zaɦranɜvat]
to say (~ thank you)	říci	[rʒiːtsi]
to scold (vt)	nadávat	[nadaːvat]
to see (vt)	vidět	[widet]

to sell (vt)	prodávat	[prodaːvat]
to send (vt)	odesílat	[odɛsiːlat]
to shoot (vi)	střílet	[strʃiːlɛt]
to shout (vi)	křičet	[krʃitʃet]
to show (vt)	ukazovat	[ukazovat]

to sign (document)	podepisovat	[podɛpisovat]
to sit down (vi)	sednout si	[sɛdnout si]
to smile (vi)	usmívat se	[usmiːvat sɛ]
to speak (vi, vt)	mluvit	[mluwit]

to steal (money, etc.)	krást	[kraːst]
to stop (cease)	zastavovat	[zastavovat]
to stop (for pause, etc.)	zastavovat se	[zastavovat sɛ]
to study (vt)	studovat	[studovat]
to swim (vi)	plavat	[plavat]

to take (vt)	brát	[braːt]
to think (vi, vt)	myslit	[mɪslit]
to threaten (vt)	vyhrožovat	[vɪɡroʒovat]
to touch (by hands)	dotýkat se	[dotiːkat sɛ]
to translate (vt)	překládat	[prʃɛklaːdat]
to trust (vt)	důvěřovat	[duːvʰerʒovat]
to try (attempt)	zkoušet	[skouʃɛt]
to turn (~ to the left)	zatáčet	[zataːtʃet]

to underestimate (vt)	podceňovat	[podtsenɜvat]
to understand (vt)	rozumět	[rozumnet]
to unite (vt)	sjednocovat	[sʰednotsovat]
to wait (vt)	čekat	[tʃekat]
to want (wish, desire)	chtít	[ɦtiːt]
to warn (vt)	upozorňovat	[upozorɲɜvat]
to work (vi)	pracovat	[pratsovat]
to write (vt)	psát	[psaːt]
to write down	zapisovat si	[zapisovat si]

14. Colours

colour	barva (f)	[barva]
shade (tint)	odstín (m)	[odstiːn]
hue	tón (m)	[toːn]
rainbow	duha (f)	[duga]

white (adj)	bílý	[biːlɪː]
black (adj)	černý	[tʃernɪː]
grey (adj)	šedý	[ʃedɪː]

green (adj)	zelený	[zɛlɛnɪ:]
yellow (adj)	žlutý	[ʒlutɪ:]
red (adj)	červený	[ʧɛrvɛnɪ:]

blue (adj)	modrý	[modrɪ:]
light blue (adj)	bledě modrý	[blɛde modrɪ:]
pink (adj)	růžový	[ru:ʒovɪ:]
orange (adj)	oranžový	[oranʒovɪ:]
violet (adj)	fialový	[fijalovɪ:]
brown (adj)	hnědý	[gnedɪ:]

| golden (adj) | zlatý | [zlatɪ:] |
| silvery (adj) | stříbřitý | [strʃi:brʒitɪ:] |

beige (adj)	béžový	[bɛ:ʒovɪ:]
cream (adj)	krémový	[krɛ:movɪ:]
turquoise (adj)	tyrkysový	[tɪrkisovɪ:]
cherry red (adj)	višňový	[wiʃnʒvɪ:]
lilac (adj)	lila	[lila]
crimson (adj)	malinový	[malinovɪ:]

light (adj)	světlý	[svʰetlɪ:]
dark (adj)	tmavý	[tmavɪ:]
bright (adj)	jasný	[jasnɪ:]

coloured (pencils)	barevný	[barɛvnɪ:]
colour (e.g. ~ film)	barevný	[barɛvnɪ:]
black-and-white (adj)	černobílý	[ʧɛrnobi:lɪ:]
plain (one colour)	jednobarevný	[jednobarɛvnɪ:]
multicoloured (adj)	různobarevný	[ru:znobarɛvnɪ:]

15. Questions

Who?	Kdo?	[gdo]
What?	Co?	[tso]
Where? (at, in)	Kde?	[gdɛ]
Where (to)?	Kam?	[kam]
Where ... from?	Odkud?	[odkud]
When?	Kdy?	[gdɪ]
Why? (aim)	Proč?	[proʧ]
Why? (reason)	Proč?	[proʧ]

What for?	Na co?	[na tso]
How? (in what way)	Jak?	[jak]
What? (which?)	Jaký?	[jakɪ:]
Which?	Který?	[ktɛrɪ:]

To whom?	Komu?	[komu]
About whom?	O kom?	[o kom]
About what?	O čem?	[o ʧem]
With whom?	S kým?	[s kɪ:m]

| How many? How much? | Kolik? | [kolik] |
| Whose? | Čí? | [ʧi:] |

16. Prepositions

with (accompanied by)	s / se	[s] / [sɛ]
without	bez	[bɛz]
to (indicating direction)	do	[do]
about (talking ~ ...)	o	[o]
before (in time)	před	[prʃɛd]
in front of ...	před	[prʃɛd]
under (beneath, below)	pod	[pod]
above (over)	nad	[nad]
on (atop)	na	[na]
from (off, out of)	z	[z]
of (made from)	z	[z]
in (e.g. ~ ten minutes)	za	[za]
over (across the top of)	přes	[prʃɛs]

17. Function words. Adverbs. Part 1

Where? (at, in)	Kde?	[gdɛ]
here (adv)	zde	[zdɛ]
there (adv)	tam	[tam]
somewhere (to be)	někde	[negdɛ]
nowhere (not anywhere)	nikde	[nigdɛ]
by (near, beside)	u ...	[u]
by the window	u okna	[u okna]
Where (to)?	Kam?	[kam]
here (e.g. come ~!)	sem	[sɛm]
there (e.g. to go ~)	tam	[tam]
from here (adv)	odsud	[odsud]
from there (adv)	odtamtud	[odtamtud]
close (adv)	blízko	[bliːzko]
far (adv)	daleko	[dalɛko]
near (e.g. ~ Paris)	kolem	[kolɛm]
nearby (adv)	nedaleko	[nɛdalɛko]
not far (adv)	nedaleko	[nɛdalɛko]
left (adj)	levý	[lɛvɪː]
on the left	zleva	[zlɛva]
to the left	vlevo	[vlɛvo]
right (adj)	pravý	[pravɪː]
on the right	zprava	[sprava]
to the right	vpravo	[vpravo]
in front (adv)	zpředu	[sprʃɛdu]
front (as adj)	přední	[prʃɛdniː]

ahead (in space)	vpřed	[vprʃɛd]
behind (adv)	za	[za]
from behind	zezadu	[zɛzadu]
back (towards the rear)	zpět	[spʰet]

| middle | střed (m) | [strʃɛd] |
| in the middle | uprostřed | [uprostrʃɛd] |

at the side	z boku	[z boku]
everywhere (adv)	všude	[vʃudɛ]
around (in all directions)	kolem	[kolɛm]

from inside	zevnitř	[zɛvnitrʃ]
somewhere (to go)	někam	[nekam]
straight (directly)	přímo	[prʃi:mo]
back (e.g. come ~)	zpět	[spʰet]

| from anywhere | odněkud | [odnekud] |
| from somewhere | odněkud | [odnekud] |

firstly (adv)	za prvé	[za prvɛ:]
secondly (adv)	za druhé	[za drugɛ:]
thirdly (adv)	za třetí	[za trʃɛti:]

suddenly (adv)	najednou	[najednou]
at first (adv)	zpočátku	[spotʃa:tku]
for the first time	poprvé	[poprvɛ:]
long before ...	dávno před ...	[da:vno prʃɛd]
anew (over again)	znovu	[znovu]
for good (adv)	navždy	[navʒdɪ]

never (adv)	nikdy	[nigdɪ]
again (adv)	opět	[opʰet]
now (adv)	nyní	[nɪni:]
often (adv)	často	[tʃasto]
then (adv)	tehdy	[tɛgdɪ]
urgently (quickly)	neodkladně	[nɛodkladne]
usually (adv)	obyčejně	[obɪtʃejne]

by the way, ...	mimochodem	[mimohodɛm]
possible (that is ~)	možná	[moʒna:]
probably (adv)	asi	[asi]
maybe (adv)	možná	[moʒna:]
besides ...	kromě toho ...	[kromne togo]
that's why ...	proto	[proto]
in spite of ...	nehledě na ...	[nɛglɛde na]
thanks to ...	díky ...	[di:kɪ]

what (pron.)	co	[tso]
that	že	[ʒe]
something	něco	[netso]
anything (something)	něco	[netso]
nothing	nic	[nits]

| who (pron.) | kdo | [gdo] |
| someone | někdo | [negdo] |

somebody	někdo	[negdo]
nobody	nikdo	[nigdo]
nowhere (a voyage to ~)	nikam	[nikam]
nobody's	ničí	[nitʃiː]
somebody's	něčí	[netʃiː]

so (I'm ~ glad)	tak	[tak]
also (as well)	také	[takɛː]
too (as well)	také	[takɛː]

18. Function words. Adverbs. Part 2

Why?	Proč?	[protʃ]
for some reason	z nějakých důvodů	[z nejakɪːɦ duːvoduː]
because ...	protože ...	[protoʒe]
for some purpose	z nějakých důvodů	[z nejakɪːɦ duːvoduː]

and	a	[a]
or	nebo	[nɛbo]
but	ale	[alɛ]
for (e.g. ~ me)	pro	[pro]

too (excessively)	příliš	[prʃiːliʃ]
only (exclusively)	jenom	[jenom]
exactly (adv)	přesně	[prʃɛsne]
about (more or less)	kolem	[kolɛm]

approximately (adv)	přibližně	[prʃibliʒne]
approximate (adj)	přibližný	[prʃibliʒnɪː]
almost (adv)	skoro	[skoro]
the rest	zbytek (m)	[zbɪtɛk]

each (adj)	každý	[kaʒdɪː]
any (no matter which)	každý	[kaʒdɪː]
many, much (a lot of)	mnoho	[mnogo]
many people	mnozí	[mnoziː]
all (everyone)	všichni	[vʃiɦni]

in exchange for ...	výměnou za ...	[vɪːmnenou za]
in exchange (adv)	místo	[miːsto]

by hand (made)	ručně	[rutʃne]
hardly (negative opinion)	sotva	[sotva]

probably (adv)	asi	[asi]
on purpose (adv)	schválně	[sɦvaːlne]
by accident (adv)	náhodou	[naːgodou]

very (adv)	velmi	[vɛlmi]
for example (adv)	například	[naprʃiːklad]
between	mezi	[mɛzi]
among	mezi	[mɛzi]
so much (such a lot)	tolik	[tolik]
especially (adv)	zejména	[zɛjmɛːna]

Basic concepts. Part 2

19. Weekdays

Monday	**pondělí** (n)	[pondeli:]
Tuesday	**úterý** (n)	[u:tɛrɪ:]
Wednesday	**středa** (f)	[strʃɛda]
Thursday	**čtvrtek** (m)	[ʧtvrtɛk]
Friday	**pátek** (m)	[pa:tɛk]
Saturday	**sobota** (f)	[sobota]
Sunday	**neděle** (f)	[nɛdelɛ]

today (adv)	**dnes**	[dnɛs]
tomorrow (adv)	**zítra**	[zi:tra]
the day after tomorrow	**pozítří**	[pozi:trʃi:]
yesterday (adv)	**včera**	[vʧera]
the day before yesterday	**předevčírem**	[prʃɛdɛvʧi:rɛm]

day	**den** (m)	[dɛn]
working day	**pracovní den** (m)	[pratsovni: dɛn]
public holiday	**sváteční den** (m)	[sva:tɛʧni: dɛn]
day off	**volno** (n)	[volno]
weekend	**víkend** (m)	[wi:kɛnd]

all day long	**celý den**	[ʦelɪ dɛn]
next day (adv)	**příští den**	[prʃi:ʃti dɛn]
two days ago	**před dvěma dny**	[prʃɛd dvʰema dnɪ]
the day before	**den předtím**	[dɛn prʃɛdti:m]
daily (adj)	**denní**	[dɛni:]
every day (adv)	**denně**	[dɛne]

week	**týden** (m)	[tɪ:dɛn]
last week (adv)	**minulý týden**	[minulɪ tɪ:dɛn]
next week (adv)	**příští týden**	[prʃi:ʃti tɪ:dɛn]
weekly (adj)	**týdenní**	[tɪ:dɛni:]
every week (adv)	**týdně**	[tɪ:dne]
twice a week	**dvakrát týdně**	[dvakra:t tɪ:dne]
every Tuesday	**každé úterý**	[kaʒdɛ: u:tɛrɪ:]

20. Hours. Day and night

morning	**ráno** (n)	[ra:no]
in the morning	**ráno**	[ra:no]
noon, midday	**poledne** (n)	[polɛdnɛ]
in the afternoon	**odpoledne**	[odpolɛdnɛ]

evening	**večer** (m)	[vɛʧer]
in the evening	**večer**	[vɛʧer]

night	noc (f)	[noʦ]
at night	v noci	[v noʦi]
midnight	půlnoc (f)	[pu:lnoʦ]

second	sekunda (f)	[sɛkunda]
minute	minuta (f)	[minuta]
hour	hodina (f)	[godina]
half an hour	půlhodina (f)	[pu:lgodina]
quarter of an hour	čtvrthodina (f)	[ʧtvrtgodina]
fifteen minutes	patnáct minut	[patna:ʦt minut]
24 hours	den a noc	[dɛn a noʦ]

sunrise	východ (m) slunce	[vɪ:ɦod slunʦe]
dawn	úsvit (m)	[u:swit]
early morning	časné ráno (n)	[ʧasnɛ: ra:no]
sunset	západ (m) slunce	[za:pat slunʦe]

early in the morning	brzy ráno	[brzɪ ra:no]
this morning	dnes ráno	[dnɛs ra:no]
tomorrow morning	zítra ráno	[zi:tra ra:no]

this afternoon	dnes odpoledne	[dnɛs odpolɛdnɛ]
in the afternoon	odpoledne	[odpolɛdnɛ]
tomorrow afternoon	zítra odpoledne	[zi:tra odpolɛdnɛ]

| tonight (this evening) | dnes večer | [dnɛs vɛʧer] |
| tomorrow night | zítra večer | [zi:tra vɛʧer] |

at 3 o'clock sharp	přesně ve tři hodiny	[prʃɛsne vɛ trʃi godinɪ]
about 4 o'clock	kolem čtyř hodin	[kolɛm ʧtɪrʒ godin]
by 12 o'clock	do dvanácti hodin	[do dvana:ʦti godin]

in 20 minutes	za dvacet minut	[za dvaʦet minut]
in an hour	za hodinu	[za godinu]
on time (adv)	včas	[vʧas]

a quarter to ...	tři čtvrtě	[trʃi ʧtvrte]
within an hour	během hodiny	[bʰegɛm godinɪ]
every 15 minutes	každých patnáct minut	[kaʒdɪ:ɦ patna:ʦt minut]
round the clock	celodenně	[ʦelodɛne]

21. Months. Seasons

January	leden (m)	[lɛdɛn]
February	únor (m)	[u:nor]
March	březen (m)	[brʒezɛn]
April	duben (m)	[dubɛn]
May	květen (m)	[kvʰetɛn]
June	červen (m)	[ʧervɛn]

July	červenec (m)	[ʧervɛnɛʦ]
August	srpen (m)	[srpɛn]
September	září (n)	[za:rʒi:]
October	říjen (m)	[rʒi:jen]

November	listopad (m)	[listopad]
December	prosinec (m)	[prosinɛʦ]
spring	jaro (n)	[jaro]
in spring	na jaře	[na jarʒe]
spring (as adj)	jarní	[jarni:]
summer	léto (n)	[lɛ:to]
in summer	v létě	[v lɛ:te]
summer (as adj)	letní	[lɛtni:]
autumn	podzim (m)	[podzim]
in autumn	na podzim	[na podzim]
autumn (as adj)	podzimní	[podzimni:]
winter	zima (f)	[zima]
in winter	v zimě	[v zimne]
winter (as adj)	zimní	[zimni:]
month	měsíc (m)	[mnesi:ʦ]
this month	tento měsíc	[tɛnto mnesi:ʦ]
next month	příští měsíc	[prʃi:ʃti: mnesi:ʦ]
last month	minulý měsíc	[minulı: mnesi:ʦ]
a month ago	před měsícem	[prʃɛd mnesi:ʦɛm]
in a month	za měsíc	[za mnesi:ʦ]
in two months	za dva měsíce	[za dva mnesi:ʦɛ]
a whole month	celý měsíc	[ʦɛli: mnesi:ʦ]
all month long	celý měsíc	[ʦɛli: mnesi:ʦ]
monthly (~ magazine)	měsíční	[mnesi:ʧni:]
monthly (adv)	každý měsíc	[kaʒdı: mnesi:ʦ]
every month	měsíčně	[mnesi:ʧne]
twice a month	dvakrát měsíčně	[dvakra:t mnesi:ʧne]
year	rok (m)	[rok]
this year	letos	[lɛtos]
next year	příští rok	[prʃi:ʃti: rok]
last year	vloni	[vloni]
a year ago	před rokem	[prʃɛd rokɛm]
in a year	za rok	[za rok]
in two years	za dva roky	[za dva rokı]
a whole year	celý rok	[ʦɛli: rok]
all year long	celý rok	[ʦɛli: rok]
every year	každý rok	[kaʒdı: rok]
annual (adj)	každoroční	[kaʒdoroʧni:]
annually (adv)	každoročně	[kaʒdoroʧne]
4 times a year	čtyřikrát za rok	[ʧtırʒikra:t za rok]
date (e.g. today's ~)	datum (n)	[datum]
date (e.g. ~ of birth)	datum (n)	[datum]
calendar	kalendář (m)	[kalɛnda:rʒ]
half a year	půl roku	[pu:l roku]
six months	půlrok (m)	[pu:lrok]

| season (summer, etc.) | období (n) | [obdobi:] |
| century | století (n) | [stolɛti:] |

22. Units of measurement

weight	váha (f)	[va:ga]
length	délka (f)	[dɛ:lka]
width	šířka (f)	[ʃi:rʃka]
height	výška (f)	[vɪ:ʃka]
depth	hloubka (f)	[gloubka]
volume	objem (m)	[obʰem]
area	plocha (f)	[ploɦa]

gram	gram (m)	[gram]
milligram	miligram (m)	[miligram]
kilogram	kilogram (m)	[kilogram]
ton	tuna (f)	[tuna]
pound	libra (f)	[libra]
ounce	unce (f)	[untse]

metre	metr (m)	[mɛtr]
millimetre	milimetr (m)	[milimɛtr]
centimetre	centimetr (m)	[tsentɪmɛtr]
kilometre	kilometr (m)	[kilomɛtr]
mile	míle (f)	[mi:lɛ]

inch	coul (m)	[tsoul]
foot	stopa (f)	[stopa]
yard	yard (m)	[jard]

| square metre | čtvereční metr (m) | [tʃtvɛrɛtʃni: mɛtr] |
| hectare | hektar (m) | [gɛktar] |

litre	litr (m)	[litr]
degree	stupeň (m)	[stupɛɲ]
volt	volt (m)	[volt]
ampere	ampér (m)	[ampɛ:r]
horsepower	koňská síla (f)	[koɲska: si:la]

quantity	množství (n)	[mnoʒstwi:]
a little bit of …	trochu …	[troɦu]
half	polovina (f)	[polowina]

| dozen | tucet (m) | [tutset] |
| piece (item) | kus (m) | [kus] |

| size | rozměr (m) | [rozmner] |
| scale (map ~) | měřítko (n) | [mnerʒi:tko] |

minimum (adj)	minimální	[minima:lni:]
the smallest (adj)	nejmenší	[nɛjmɛnʃi:]
medium (adj)	střední	[strʃɛdni:]
maximum (adj)	maximální	[maksima:lni:]
the largest (adj)	největší	[nɛjvʰetʃi:]

27

23. Containers

jar (glass)	sklenice (f)	[sklɛnitse]
tin, can	plechovka (f)	[plɛɦovka]
bucket	vědro (n)	[vʰedro]
barrel	sud (m)	[sud]

basin (for washing)	mísa (f)	[mi:sa]
tank (for liquid, gas)	nádrž (f)	[na:drʒ]
hip flask	plochá láhev (f)	[ploɦa: la:gɛv]
jerrycan	kanystr (m)	[kanıstr]
cistern (tank)	cisterna (f)	[tsıstɛrna]

mug	hrníček (m)	[grni:t͡ʃek]
cup (of coffee, etc.)	šálek (m)	[ʃa:lɛk]
saucer	talířek (m)	[tali:rʒek]
glass (tumbler)	sklenice (f)	[sklɛnitse]
glass (~ of vine)	sklenka (f)	[sklɛŋka]
stew pot	hrnec (m)	[grnɛts]

| bottle (~ of wine) | láhev (f) | [la:gɛv] |
| neck (of the bottle) | hrdlo (n) | [grdlo] |

carafe	karafa (f)	[karafa]
jug (earthenware)	džbán (m)	[dʒba:n]
vessel (container)	nádoba (f)	[na:doba]
pot (crock)	hrnec (m)	[grnɛts]
vase	váza (f)	[va:za]

bottle (~ of perfume)	flakón (m)	[flako:n]
vial, small bottle	lahvička (f)	[lagwit͡ʃka]
tube (of toothpaste)	tuba (f)	[tuba]

sack (bag)	pytel (m)	[pıtɛl]
bag (paper ~, plastic ~)	sáček (m)	[sa:t͡ʃek]
packet (of cigarettes, etc.)	balíček (m)	[bali:t͡ʃek]

box (e.g. shoebox)	krabice (f)	[krabitse]
crate	schránka (f)	[sɦra:ŋka]
basket	koš (m)	[koʃ]

HUMAN BEING

Human being. The body

24. Head

head	**hlava** (f)	[glava]
face	**obličej** (f)	[oblitʃej]
nose	**nos** (m)	[nos]
mouth	**ústa** (n pl)	[uːsta]
eye	**oko** (n)	[oko]
eyes	**oči** (n pl)	[otʃi]
pupil	**zornice** (f)	[zornitse]
eyebrow	**obočí** (n)	[obotʃiː]
eyelash	**řasa** (f)	[rʒasa]
eyelid	**víčko** (n)	[wiːtʃko]
tongue	**jazyk** (m)	[jazɪk]
tooth	**zub** (m)	[zub]
lips	**rty** (m pl)	[rtɪ]
cheekbones	**lícní kosti** (f pl)	[liːtsni: kosti]
gum	**dáseň** (f)	[daːsɛɲ]
palate	**patro** (n)	[patro]
nostrils	**chřípí** (n)	[ɦrʃiːpiː]
chin	**brada** (f)	[brada]
jaw	**čelist** (f)	[tʃelist]
cheek	**tvář** (f)	[tvaːrʒ]
forehead	**čelo** (n)	[tʃelo]
temple	**spánek** (n)	[spaːnɛk]
ear	**ucho** (n)	[uɦo]
back of the head	**týl** (m)	[tɪːl]
neck	**krk** (m)	[krk]
throat	**hrdlo** (n)	[grdlo]
hair	**vlasy** (m pl)	[vlasɪ]
hairstyle	**účes** (m)	[uːtʃes]
haircut	**střih** (m)	[strʃiɦ]
wig	**paruka** (f)	[paruka]
moustache	**vousy** (m pl)	[vousɪ]
beard	**plnovous** (m)	[plnovous]
to have (a beard, etc.)	**nosit**	[nosit]
plait	**cop** (m)	[tsop]
sideboards	**licousy** (m pl)	[litsousɪ]
red-haired (adj)	**zrzavý**	[zrzavɪː]
grey (hair)	**šedivý**	[ʃedivɪː]

| bald (adj) | lysý | [lɪsɪ:] |
| bald patch | lysina (f) | [lɪsina] |

| ponytail | ocas (m) | [oʦas] |
| fringe | ofina (f) | [ofina] |

25. Human body

| hand | ruka (f) | [ruka] |
| arm | ruka (f) | [ruka] |

finger	prst (m)	[prst]
thumb	palec (m)	[palɛʦ]
little finger	malíček (m)	[mali:ʧek]
nail	nehet (m)	[nɛgɛt]

fist	pěst (f)	[pʰest]
palm	dlaň (f)	[dlaɲ]
wrist	zápěstí (n)	[za:pɛsti:]
forearm	předloktí (n)	[prʃɛdlokti:]
elbow	loket (m)	[lokɛt]
shoulder	rameno (n)	[ramɛno]

leg	noha (f)	[noga]
foot	chodidlo (n)	[ɦodidlo]
knee	koleno (n)	[kolɛno]
calf (part of leg)	lýtko (n)	[lɪ:tko]
hip	stehno (n)	[stɛgno]
heel	pata (f)	[pata]

body	tělo (n)	[telo]
stomach	břicho (n)	[brʒiɦo]
chest	prsa (n pl)	[prsa]
breast	prs (m)	[prs]
flank	bok (m)	[bok]
back	záda (n pl)	[za:da]
lower back	kříž (m)	[krʃi:ʒ]
waist	pás (m)	[pa:s]

navel	pupek (m)	[pupɛk]
buttocks	hýždě (f pl)	[gɪ:ʒde]
bottom	zadek (m)	[zadɛk]

beauty mark	mateřské znaménko (n)	[matɛrʃkɛ: znamɛ:ŋko]
tattoo	tetování (n)	[tɛtova:ni:]
scar	jizva (f)	[jɪzva]

Clothing & Accessories

26. Outerwear. Coats

clothes	oblečení (n)	[oblɛtʃeni:]
outer clothing	svrchní oděv (m)	[svrɦni: odev]
winter clothing	zimní oděv (m)	[zimni: odev]
overcoat	kabát (m)	[kaba:t]
fur coat	kožich (m)	[koʒiɦ]
fur jacket	krátký kožich (m)	[kra:tkɪ: koʒiɦ]
down coat	peřová bunda (f)	[pɛrʒova: bunda]
jacket (e.g. leather ~)	bunda (f)	[bunda]
raincoat	plášť (m)	[pla:ʃtʲ]
waterproof (adj)	nepromokavý	[nɛpromokavɪ:]

27. Men's & women's clothing

shirt	košile (f)	[koʃilɛ]
trousers	kalhoty (f pl)	[kalgotɪ]
jeans	džínsy (m pl)	[dʒi:nsɪ]
jacket (of man's suit)	sako (n)	[sako]
suit	pánský oblek (m)	[pa:nskɪ: oblɛk]
dress (frock)	šaty (m pl)	[ʃatɪ]
skirt	sukně (f)	[suknɛ]
blouse	blůzka (f)	[blu:zka]
knitted jacket	svetr (m)	[svɛtr]
jacket (of woman's suit)	žaket (m)	[ʒakɛt]
T-shirt	tričko (n)	[tritʃko]
shorts (short trousers)	šortky (f pl)	[ʃortkɪ]
tracksuit	teplákova souprava (f)	[tɛpla:kova: souprava]
bathrobe	župan (m)	[ʒupan]
pyjamas	pyžamo (n)	[piʒamo]
sweater	svetr (m)	[svɛtr]
pullover	pulovr (m)	[pulovr]
waistcoat	vesta (f)	[vɛsta]
tailcoat	frak (m)	[frak]
dinner suit	smoking (m)	[smokiŋ]
uniform	uniforma (f)	[unɪforma]
workwear	pracovní oděv (m)	[pratsovni: odev]
boiler suit	kombinéza (f)	[kombinɛ:za]
coat (e.g. doctor's ~)	plášť (m)	[pla:ʃtʲ]

28. Clothing. Underwear

underwear	spodní prádlo (n)	[spodni: pra:dlo]
vest (singlet)	tílko (n)	[tilko]
socks	ponožky (f pl)	[ponoʒkɪ]

nightgown	noční košile (f)	[notʃni: koʃilɛ]
bra	podprsenka (f)	[podprsɛŋka]
knee highs	podkolenky (f pl)	[podkolɛŋkɪ]
tights	punčochové kalhoty (f pl)	[puntʃoɦovɛ: kalgotɪ]
stockings	punčochy (f pl)	[puntʃoɦɪ]
swimsuit, bikini	plavky (f pl)	[plavkɪ]

29. Headwear

hat	čepice (f)	[tʃepitse]
trilby hat	klobouk (m)	[klobouk]
baseball cap	kšiltovka (f)	[kʃiltovka]
flatcap	čepice (f)	[tʃepitse]

beret	baret (m)	[barɛt]
hood	kapuce (f)	[kaputse]
panama	panamský klobouk (m)	[panamskɪ: klobouk]
knitted hat	pletená čepice (f)	[plɛtɛna: tʃepitse]

headscarf	šátek (m)	[ʃa:tɛk]
women's hat	klobouček (m)	[kloboutʃek]

hard hat	přilba (f)	[prʃilba]
forage cap	lodička (f)	[loditʃka]
helmet	helma (f)	[gɛlma]

bowler	tvrďák (m)	[tvrdʲa:k]
top hat	válec (m)	[va:lɛts]

30. Footwear

footwear	obuv (f)	[obuv]
ankle boots	boty (f pl)	[botɪ]
shoes (low-heeled ~)	střevíce (m pl)	[strʃɛwi:tse]
boots (cowboy ~)	holínky (f pl)	[goli:ŋkɪ]
slippers	bačkory (f pl)	[batʃkorɪ]

trainers	tenisky (f pl)	[tɛnɪskɪ]
plimsolls, pumps	kecky (f pl)	[kɛtskɪ]
sandals	sandály (m pl)	[sanda:lɪ]

cobbler	obuvník (m)	[obuvni:k]
heel	podpatek (m)	[podpatɛk]
pair (of shoes)	pár (m)	[pa:r]
shoelace	tkanička (f)	[tkanitʃka]

to lace up (vt)	šněrovat	[ʃnerovat]
shoehorn	lžíce (f) na boty	[ʒiːtse na botı]
shoe polish	krém (m) na boty	[krɛːm na botı]

31. Personal accessories

gloves	rukavice (f pl)	[rukawitse]
mittens	palčáky (m pl)	[paltʃaːkı]
scarf (long)	šála (f)	[ʃaːla]

glasses	brýle (f pl)	[brıːlɛ]
frame (eyeglass ~)	obroučky (m pl)	[obroutʃkı]
umbrella	deštník (m)	[dɛʃtniːk]
walking stick	hůl (f)	[guːl]
hairbrush	kartáč (m) na vlasy	[kartaːtʃ na vlası]
fan	vějíř (m)	[vʰejıːrʒ]

tie (necktie)	kravata (f)	[kravata]
bow tie	motýlek (m)	[motıːlɛk]
braces	šle (f pl)	[ʃlɛ]
handkerchief	kapesník (m)	[kapesniːk]

comb	hřeben (m)	[grʒebɛn]
hair slide	sponka (f)	[spoŋka]
hairpin	vlásnička (f)	[vlaːsnitʃka]
buckle	spona (f)	[spona]

| belt | pás (m) | [paːs] |
| shoulder strap | řemen (m) | [rʒemɛn] |

bag (handbag)	taška (f)	[taʃka]
handbag	kabelka (f)	[kabɛlka]
rucksack	batoh (m)	[batoɦ]

32. Clothing. Miscellaneous

fashion	móda (f)	[moːda]
in vogue (adj)	módní	[moːdniː]
fashion designer	modelář (m)	[modɛlaːrʒ]

collar	límec (m)	[liːmɛts]
pocket	kapsa (f)	[kapsa]
pocket (as adj)	kapesní	[kapɛsniː]
sleeve	rukáv (m)	[rukaːv]
hanging loop	poutko (n)	[poutko]
flies (on trousers)	poklopec (m)	[poklopɛts]

zip (fastener)	zip (m)	[zip]
fastener	spona (f)	[spona]
button	knoflík (m)	[knofliːk]
buttonhole	dírka (f)	[diːrka]
to come off (ab. button)	utrhnout se	[utrgnout sɛ]

to sew (vi, vt)	šít	[ʃiːt]
to embroider (vi, vt)	vyšívat	[vɪʃiːvat]
embroidery	výšivka (f)	[vɪːʃivka]
sewing needle	jehla (f)	[jegla]
thread	nit (f)	[nit]
seam	šev (m)	[ʃɛv]

to get dirty (vi)	ušpinit se	[uʃpinit sɛ]
stain (mark, spot)	skvrna (f)	[skvrna]
to crease, crumple (vi)	pomačkat se	[pomatʃkat sɛ]
to tear (vt)	roztrhat	[roztrgat]
clothes moth	mol (m)	[mol]

33. Personal care. Cosmetics

toothpaste	zubní pasta (f)	[zubniː pasta]
toothbrush	kartáček (m) na zuby	[kartaːtʃek na zubɪ]
to clean one's teeth	čistit si zuby	[tʃistit si zubɪ]

razor	holicí strojek (m)	[golitsi strojek]
shaving cream	krém (m) na holení	[krɛːm na golɛni:]
to shave (vi)	holit se	[golit sɛ]

| soap | mýdlo (n) | [mɪːdlo] |
| shampoo | šampon (m) | [ʃampon] |

scissors	nůžky (f pl)	[nuːʒkɪ]
nail file	pilník (m) na nehty	[pilni:k na nɛɦtɪ]
nail clippers	kleštičky (f pl) na nehty	[klɛʃtiʧkɪ na nɛɦtɪ]
tweezers	pinzeta (f)	[pinzeta]

cosmetics	kosmetika (f)	[kosmɛtɪka]
face pack	kosmetická maska (f)	[kosmɛtitska: maska]
manicure	manikúra (f)	[manɪku:ra]
to have a manicure	dělat manikúru	[delat manɪku:ru]
pedicure	pedikúra (f)	[pɛdɪku:ra]

make-up bag	kosmetická kabelka (f)	[kosmɛtitska: kabɛlka]
face powder	pudr (m)	[pudr]
powder compact	pudřenka (f)	[pudrʒeŋka]
blusher	červené líčidlo (n)	[tʃervɛnɛ: liːtʃidlo]

perfume (bottled)	voňavka (f)	[voɲavka]
toilet water	toaletní voda (f)	[toalɛtni: voda]
lotion	pleťová voda (f)	[plɛtʒva: voda]
cologne	kolínská voda (f)	[koli:nska: voda]

eyeshadow	oční stíny (m pl)	[otʃni: sti:nɪ]
eyeliner	tužka (f) na oči	[tuʒka na otʃi]
mascara	řasenka (f)	[rʒasɛŋka]

lipstick	rtěnka (f)	[rteŋka]
nail polish	lak (m) na nehty	[lak na nɛɦtɪ]
hair spray	lak (m) na vlasy	[lak na vlasɪ]

deodorant	deodorant (m)	[dɛodorant]
cream	krém (m)	[krɛ:m]
face cream	pleťový krém (m)	[plɛtɔvɪ: krɛ:m]
hand cream	krém (m) na ruce	[krɛ:m na rutse]
anti-wrinkle cream	krém (m) proti vráskám	[krɛ:m proti vra:ska:m]
day (as adj)	denní	[dɛni:]
night (as adj)	noční	[notʃni:]

tampon	tampón (m)	[tampo:n]
toilet paper	toaletní papír (m)	[toalɛtni: papi:r]
hair dryer	fén (m)	[fɛ:n]

34. Watches. Clocks

watch (wristwatch)	hodinky (f pl)	[godiŋkɪ]
dial	ciferník (m)	[tsifɛrni:k]
hand (of clock, watch)	ručička (f)	[rutʃitʃka]
metal bracelet	náramek (m)	[na:ramɛk]
watch strap	pásek (m)	[pa:sɛk]

battery	baterka (f)	[batɛrka]
to be flat (battery)	vybít se	[vɪbi:t sɛ]
to change a battery	vyměnit baterku	[vɪmnenit batɛrku]
to run fast	jít napřed	[jɪ:t naprʃɛd]
to run slow	opožďovat se	[opoʒdɔvat sɛ]

wall clock	nástěnné hodiny (f pl)	[na:stɛɲɛ: godinɪ]
hourglass	přesýpací hodiny (f pl)	[prʃɛsɪ:patsi: godinɪ]
sundial	sluneční hodiny (f pl)	[slunɛtʃni: godinɪ]
alarm clock	budík (m)	[budi:k]
watchmaker	hodinář (m)	[godina:rʒ]
to repair (vt)	opravovat	[opravovat]

Food. Nutricion

35. Food

meat	maso (n)	[maso]
chicken	slepice (f)	[slɛpitse]
young chicken	kuře (n)	[kurʒe]
duck	kachna (f)	[kaɦna]
goose	husa (f)	[gusa]
game	zvěřina (f)	[zwerʒina]
turkey	krůta (f)	[kru:ta]

pork	vepřové (n)	[vɛprʃovɛ:]
veal	telecí (n)	[tɛlɛtsi:]
lamb	skopové (n)	[skopovɛ:]
beef	hovězí (n)	[govʰezi:]
rabbit	králík (m)	[kra:li:k]

sausage (salami, etc.)	salám (m)	[sala:m]
vienna sausage	párek (m)	[pa:rɛk]
bacon	slanina (f)	[slanina]
ham	šunka (f)	[ʃuŋka]
gammon (ham)	kýta (f)	[kɪ:ta]

pâté	paštika (f)	[paʃtika]
liver	játra (n pl)	[ja:tra]
lard	sádlo (n)	[sa:dlo]
mince	mleté maso (n)	[mlɛtɛ: maso]
tongue	jazyk (m)	[jazɪk]

egg	vejce (n)	[vɛjtse]
eggs	vejce (n pl)	[vɛjtse]
egg white	bílek (m)	[bi:lɛk]
egg yolk	žloutek (m)	[ʒloutɛk]

fish	ryby (f pl)	[rɪbɪ]
seafood	mořské plody (m pl)	[morʃskɛ: plodɪ]
caviar	kaviár (m)	[kawija:r]

crab	krab (m)	[krab]
prawn	kreveta (f)	[krɛvɛta]
oyster	ústřice (f)	[u:strʃitse]
spiny lobster	langusta (f)	[laŋusta]
octopus	chobotnice (f)	[ɦobotnitse]
squid	sépie (f)	[sɛ:pije]

sturgeon	jeseter (m)	[jesɛtɛr]
salmon	losos (m)	[losos]
halibut	platýs (m)	[platɪ:s]
cod	treska (f)	[trɛska]

mackerel	makrela (f)	[makrɛla]
tuna	tuňák (m)	[tuɲaːk]
eel	úhoř (m)	[uːgorʒ]

trout	pstruh (m)	[pstruɦ]
sardine	sardinka (f)	[sardɪŋka]
pike	štika (f)	[ʃtika]
herring	sled' (f)	[slɛdʲ]

bread	chléb (m)	[ɦlɛːb]
cheese	sýr (m)	[sɪːr]
sugar	cukr (m)	[tsukr]
salt	sůl (f)	[suːl]

rice	rýže (f)	[rɪːʒe]
pasta	makaróny (m pl)	[makaroːnɪ]
noodles	nudle (f pl)	[nudlɛ]

butter	máslo (n)	[maːslo]
vegetable oil	olej (m)	[olɛj]
sunflower oil	slunečnicový olej (m)	[slunɛtʃɲitsovɪː olɛj]
margarine	margarín (m)	[margariːn]

| olives | olivy (f) | [olivɪ] |
| olive oil | olivový olej (m) | [olivovɪː olɛj] |

milk	mléko (n)	[mlɛːko]
condensed milk	kondenzované mléko (n)	[kondɛnzovanɛː mlɛːko]
yogurt	jogurt (m)	[jogurt]
sour cream	kyselá smetana (f)	[kɪsɛlaː smɛtana]
cream (of milk)	sladká smetana (f)	[sladkaː smɛtana]

| mayonnaise | majonéza (f) | [majonɛːza] |
| buttercream | krém (m) | [krɛːm] |

groats	kroupy (f pl)	[kroupɪ]
flour	mouka (f)	[mouka]
tinned food	konzerva (f)	[konzɛrva]

cornflakes	kukuřičné vločky (f pl)	[kukurʒitʃnɛː vlotʃkɪ]
honey	med (m)	[mɛd]
jam	džem (m)	[dʒem]
chewing gum	žvýkačka (f)	[ʒvɪːkatʃka]

36. Drinks

water	voda (f)	[voda]
drinking water	pitná voda (f)	[pitnaː voda]
mineral water	minerálka (f)	[minɛraːlka]

still (adj)	neperlivý	[nɛpɛrlivɪː]
carbonated (adj)	perlivý	[pɛrlivɪː]
sparkling (adj)	perlivý	[pɛrlivɪː]
ice	led (m)	[lɛd]

with ice	s ledem	[s lɛdɛm]
non-alcoholic (adj)	nealkoholický	[nɛalkogolitskɪ:]
soft drink	nealkoholický nápoj (m)	[nɛalkogolitskɪ: na:poj]
cool soft drink	osvěžující nápoj (m)	[osvʰeʒujɪːtsi: na:poj]
lemonade	limonáda (f)	[limona:da]

spirits	alkoholické nápoje (m pl)	[alkogolitskɛ: na:poje]
wine	víno (n)	[wi:no]
white wine	bílé víno (n)	[bi:lɛ: wi:no]
red wine	červené víno (n)	[tʃervɛnɛ: wi:no]

liqueur	likér (m)	[likɛ:r]
champagne	šampaňské (n)	[ʃampaɲskɛ:]
vermouth	vermut (m)	[vɛrmut]

whisky	whisky (f)	[wiski]
vodka	vodka (f)	[vodka]
gin	džin (m)	[dʒin]
cognac	koňak (m)	[koɲak]
rum	rum (m)	[rum]

coffee	káva (f)	[ka:va]
black coffee	černá káva (f)	[tʃerna: ka:va]
white coffee	bílá káva (f)	[bi:la: ka:va]
cappuccino	kapučíno (n)	[kaputʃi:no]
instant coffee	rozpustná káva (f)	[rozpustna: ka:va]

milk	mléko (n)	[mlɛ:ko]
cocktail	koktail (m)	[koktajl]
milk shake	mléčný koktail (m)	[mlɛtʃnɪ: koktajl]

juice	šťáva (f)	[ʃtʲa:va]
tomato juice	rajčatová šťáva (f)	[rajtʃatova: ʃtʲa:va]
orange juice	pomerančový džus (m)	[pomɛrantʃovɪ: dʒus]
freshly squeezed juice	vymačkaná šťáva (f)	[vɪmatʃkana: ʃtʲa:va]

beer	pivo (n)	[pivo]
lager	světlé pivo (n)	[svʰetlɛ: pivo]
bitter	tmavé pivo (n)	[tmavɛ: pivo]

tea	čaj (m)	[tʃaj]
black tea	černý čaj (m)	[tʃernɪ: tʃaj]
green tea	zelený čaj (m)	[zɛlɛnɪ: tʃaj]

37. Vegetables

| vegetables | zelenina (f) | [zɛlɛnina] |
| greens | zelenina (f) | [zɛlɛnina] |

tomato	rajské jablíčko (n)	[rajskɛ: jabli:tʃko]
cucumber	okurka (f)	[okurka]
carrot	mrkev (f)	[mrkɛv]
potato	brambory (f pl)	[bramborɪ]
onion	cibule (f)	[tsibulɛ]

garlic	česnek (m)	[ʧesnɛk]
cabbage	zelí (n)	[zɛli:]
cauliflower	květák (m)	[kvʰeta:k]
Brussels sprouts	růžičková kapusta (f)	[ru:ʒiʧkova: kapusta]
broccoli	brokolice (f)	[brokoliʦe]

beetroot	červená řepa (f)	[ʧerwena: rʒepa]
aubergine	lilek (m)	[lilɛk]
marrow	cukina, cuketa (f)	[ʦukina], [ʦuketa]
pumpkin	tykev (f)	[tɪkɛf]
turnip	vodní řepa (f)	[vodni: rʒepa]

parsley	petržel (f)	[pɛtrʒel]
dill	kopr (m)	[kopr]
lettuce	salát (m)	[sala:t]
celery	celer (m)	[ʦelɛr]
asparagus	chřest (m)	[hrʃɛst]
spinach	špenát (m)	[ʃpɛna:t]

pea	hrách (m)	[gra:ɦ]
beans	boby (m pl)	[bobɪ]
maize	kukuřice (f)	[kukurʒiʦe]
kidney bean	fazole (f)	[fazolɛ]

bell pepper	pepř (m)	[pɛprʃ]
radish	ředkvička (f)	[rʒedkwiʧka]
artichoke	artyčok (m)	[artɪʧok]

38. Fruits. Nuts

fruit	ovoce (n)	[ovoʦe]
apple	jablko (n)	[jablko]
pear	hruška (f)	[gruʃka]
lemon	citrón (m)	[ʦitro:n]
orange	pomeranč (m)	[pomɛranʧ]
strawberry	zahradní jahody (f pl)	[zagradni: jagodɪ]

tangerine	mandarinka (f)	[mandariŋka]
plum	švestka (f)	[ʃvɛstka]
peach	broskev (f)	[broskɛv]
apricot	meruňka (f)	[mɛruɲka]
raspberry	maliny (f pl)	[malinɪ]
pineapple	ananas (m)	[ananas]

banana	banán (m)	[bana:n]
watermelon	vodní meloun (m)	[vodni: mɛloun]
grape	hroznové víno (n)	[groznovɛ: wi:no]
sour cherry	višně (f)	[wiʃne]
sweet cherry	třešně (f)	[trʃɛʃne]
melon	cukrový meloun (m)	[ʦukrovɪ mɛloun]

grapefruit	grapefruit (m)	[grɛjpfru:t]
avocado	avokádo (n)	[avoka:do]
papaya	papája (f)	[papa:ja]

| mango | mango (n) | [maŋo] |
| pomegranate | granátové jablko (n) | [grana:tovɛ: jablko] |

redcurrant	červený rybíz (m)	[ʧervɛnɪ: rɪbi:z]
blackcurrant	černý rybíz (m)	[ʧernɪ: rɪbi:z]
gooseberry	angrešt (m)	[aŋrɛʃt]
bilberry	borůvky (f pl)	[boru:vkɪ]
blackberry	ostružiny (f pl)	[ostruʒɪnɪ]

raisin	hrozinky (f pl)	[grozɪŋkɪ]
fig	fík (m)	[fi:k]
date	datle (f)	[datlɛ]

peanut	bursý oříšek (m)	[burskɪ: orʒi:ʃɛk]
almond	mandle (f)	[mandlɛ]
walnut	vlašský ořech (m)	[vlaʃskɪ: orʒeñ]
hazelnut	lískový ořech (m)	[li:skovɪ: orʒeñ]
coconut	kokos (m)	[kokos]
pistachios	pistácie (f)	[pista:ʦije]

39. Bread. Sweets

confectionery (pastry)	cukroví (n)	[ʦukrowi:]
bread	chléb (m)	[ɦlɛ:b]
biscuits	sušenky (f pl)	[suʃɛŋkɪ]

chocolate (n)	čokoláda (f)	[ʧokola:da]
chocolate (as adj)	čokoládový	[ʧokola:dovɪ:]
sweet	bonbón (m)	[bonbo:n]
cake (e.g. cupcake)	zákusek (m)	[za:kusɛk]
cake (e.g. birthday ~)	dort (m)	[dort]

| pie (e.g. apple ~) | koláč (m) | [kola:ʧ] |
| filling (for cake, pie) | nádivka (f) | [na:divka] |

whole fruit jam	zavařenina (f)	[zavarʒenina]
marmalade	marmeláda (f)	[marmɛla:da]
waffle	oplatky (pl)	[oplatkɪ]
ice-cream	zmrzlina (f)	[zmrzlina]

40. Cooked dishes

course, dish	jídlo (n)	[ji:dlo]
cuisine	kuchyně (f)	[kuɦɪne]
recipe	recept (m)	[rɛʦept]
portion	porce (f)	[porʦe]

| salad | salát (m) | [sala:t] |
| soup | polévka (f) | [polɛ:vka] |

| clear soup (broth) | vývar (m) | [vɪ:var] |
| sandwich (bread) | obložený chlebíček (m) | [obloʒenɪ: ɦlɛbi:ʧek] |

fried eggs	míchaná vejce (n pl)	[miːɦana: vɛjtse]
cutlet	kotleta (f)	[kotlɛta]
hamburger (beefburger)	hamburger (m)	[gamburgɛr]
beefsteak	biftek (m)	[biftɛk]
roast meat	pečeně (f)	[pɛtʃenɛ]

garnish	příloha (f)	[prʃiːloga]
spaghetti	spagety (m pl)	[spagɛtɪ]
mash	bramborová kaše (f)	[bramborova: kaʃɛ]
pizza	pizza (f)	[pitsa]
porridge (oatmeal, etc.)	kaše (f)	[kaʃɛ]
omelette	omeleta (f)	[omɛlɛta]

boiled (e.g. ~ beef)	vařený	[varʒenɪ:]
smoked (adj)	uzený	[uzɛnɪ:]
fried (adj)	smažený	[smaʒenɪ:]
dried (adj)	sušený	[suʃɛnɪ:]
frozen (adj)	zmražený	[zmraʒenɪ:]
pickled (adj)	marinovaný	[marinovanɪ:]

sweet (sugary)	sladký	[sladkɪ:]
salty (adj)	slaný	[slanɪ:]
cold (adj)	studený	[studɛnɪ:]
hot (adj)	teplý	[tɛplɪ:]
bitter (adj)	hořký	[gorʃkɪ:]
tasty (adj)	chutný	[ɦutnɪ:]

to cook (in boiling water)	vařit	[varʒit]
to cook (dinner)	vařit	[varʒit]
to fry (vt)	smažit	[smaʒit]
to heat up (food)	ohřívat	[ogrʒiːvat]

to salt (vt)	solit	[solit]
to pepper (vt)	pepřit	[pɛprʃit]
to grate (vt)	strouhat	[strougat]
peel (n)	slupka (f)	[slupka]
to peel (vt)	loupat	[loupat]

41. Spices

salt	sůl (f)	[suːl]
salty (adj)	slaný	[slanɪ:]
to salt (vt)	solit	[solit]

black pepper	pepř (m)	[pɛprʃ]
red pepper	červená paprika (f)	[tʃɛrvɛna: paprika]
mustard	hořčice (f)	[gorʃtʃitse]
horseradish	křen (m)	[krʃɛn]

condiment	koření (n)	[korʒeni:]
spice	koření (n)	[korʒeni:]
sauce	omáčka (f)	[oma:tʃka]
vinegar	ocet (m)	[otset]
anise	anýz (m)	[anɪ:z]

basil	bazalka (f)	[bazalka]
cloves	hřebíček (m)	[grʒebiːʧek]
ginger	zázvor (m)	[zaːzvor]
coriander	koriandr (m)	[korijandr]
cinnamon	skořice (f)	[skorʒiʦe]

sesame	sezam (m)	[sɛzam]
bay leaf	bobkový list (m)	[bobkovːː list]
paprika	paprika (f)	[paprika]
caraway	kmín (m)	[kmiːn]
saffron	šafrán (m)	[ʃafraːn]

42. Meals

| food | jídlo (n) | [jːːdlo] |
| to eat (vi, vt) | jíst | [jːːst] |

breakfast	snídaně (f)	[sniːdane]
to have breakfast	snídat	[sniːdat]
lunch	oběd (m)	[obʰed]
to have lunch	obědvat	[obʰedvat]
dinner	večeře (f)	[vɛʧerʒe]
to have dinner	večeřet	[vɛʧerʒet]

| appetite | chuť (f) k jídlu (n) | [ɦutⁱ k jːːdlu] |
| Enjoy your meal! | Dobrou chuť! | [dobrou ɦutⁱ] |

to open (~ a bottle)	otvírat	[otwiːrat]
to spill (liquid)	rozlít	[rozliːt]
to spill out (vi)	rozlít se	[rozliːt sɛ]

to boil (vi)	vřít	[vrʒiːt]
to boil (vt)	vařit	[varʒit]
boiled (~ water)	svařený	[svarʒenːː]
to cool (vt)	ochladit	[oɦladit]
to cool down (vi)	ochlazovat se	[oɦlazovat sɛ]

| taste, flavour | chuť (f) | [ɦutⁱ] |
| aftertaste | příchuť (f) | [prʃiːɦutⁱ] |

to be on a diet	držet dietu	[drʒet dijetu]
diet	dieta (f)	[dijeta]
vitamin	vitamín (m)	[witamiːn]
calorie	kalorie (f)	[kalorije]

| vegetarian (n) | vegetarián (m) | [vɛgɛtarijaːn] |
| vegetarian (adj) | vegetariánský | [vɛgɛtarijaːnskːː] |

fats (nutrient)	tuky (m)	[tuki]
proteins	bílkoviny (f)	[biːlkowinːː]
carbohydrates	kysličník (m) uhličitý	[kːːsliʧniːk ugliʧitːː]
slice (of lemon, ham)	plátek (m)	[plaːtɛk]
piece (of cake, pie)	kousek (m)	[kousɛk]
crumb (of bread)	drobek (m)	[drobɛk]

43. Table setting

spoon	lžíce (f)	[ʒi:ʦe]
knife	nůž (m)	[nu:ʒ]
fork	vidlička (f)	[widliʧka]
cup (of coffee)	šálek (m)	[ʃa:lɛk]
plate (dinner ~)	talíř (m)	[tali:rʒ]
saucer	talířek (m)	[tali:rʒek]
serviette	ubrousek (m)	[ubrousɛk]
toothpick	párátko (n)	[pa:ra:tko]

44. Restaurant

restaurant	restaurace (f)	[rɛstauraʦe]
coffee bar	kavárna (f)	[kava:rna]
pub, bar	bar (m)	[bar]
tearoom	čajovna (f)	[ʧajovna]
waiter	číšník (m)	[ʧi:ʃni:k]
waitress	číšnice (f)	[ʧi:ʃniʦe]
barman	barman (m)	[barman]
menu	jídelní lístek (m)	[jɪ:dɛlni: li:stɛk]
wine list	nápojový lístek (m)	[na:pojovɪ: li:stɛk]
to book a table	rezervovat stůl	[rɛzɛrvovat stu:l]
course, dish	jídlo (n)	[jɪ:dlo]
to order (meal)	objednat si	[obʰednat si]
to make an order	objednat si	[obʰednat si]
aperitif	aperitiv (m)	[apɛritɪv]
starter	předkrm (m)	[prʃɛdkrm]
dessert, sweet	desert (m)	[dɛsɛrt]
bill	účet (m)	[u:ʧet]
to pay the bill	zaplatit účet	[zaplatit u:ʧet]
to give change	dát nazpátek	[da:t naspa:tɛk]
tip	spropitné (n)	[spropitnɛ:]

Family, relatives and friends

45. Personal information. Forms

name, first name	jméno (n)	[jmɛ:no]
family name	příjmení (n)	[prʃi:jmɛni:]
date of birth	datum (n) narození	[datum narozɛni:]
place of birth	místo (n) narození	[mi:sto narozɛni:]
nationality	národnost (f)	[na:rodnost]
place of residence	bydliště (n)	[bɪdliʃte]
country	země (f)	[zɛmne]
profession (occupation)	povolání (n)	[povola:ni:]
gender, sex	pohlaví (n)	[poglawi:]
height	postava (f)	[postava]
weight	váha (f)	[va:ga]

46. Family members. Relatives

mother	matka (f)	[matka]
father	otec (m)	[otɛts]
son	syn (m)	[sɪn]
daughter	dcera (f)	[dtsera]
younger daughter	nejmladší dcera (f)	[nɛjmladʃi: dtsera]
younger son	nejmladší syn (m)	[nɛjmladʃi: sɪn]
eldest daughter	nejstarší dcera (f)	[nɛjstarʃi: dtsera]
eldest son	nejstarší syn (m)	[nɛjstarʃi: sɪn]
brother	bratr (m)	[bratr]
sister	sestra (f)	[sɛstra]
cousin (masc.)	bratranec (m)	[bratranɛts]
cousin (fem.)	sestřenice (f)	[sɛstrʃɛnitse]
mummy	maminka (f)	[maminka]
dad, daddy	táta (m)	[ta:ta]
parents	rodiče (m pl)	[roditʃe]
child	dítě (n)	[di:te]
children	děti (f pl)	[deti]
grandmother	babička (f)	[babitʃka]
grandfather	dědeček (m)	[dedɛtʃek]
grandson	vnuk (m)	[vnuk]
granddaughter	vnučka (f)	[vnutʃka]
grandchildren	vnuci (m pl)	[vnutsi]
uncle	strýc (m)	[strɪ:ts]
aunt	teta (f)	[tɛta]

| nephew | synovec (m) | [sɪnovɛts] |
| niece | neteř (f) | [nɛtɛrʒ] |

mother-in-law	tchyně (f)	[tɦɪne]
father-in-law	tchán (m)	[tɦa:n]
son-in-law	zeť (m)	[zɛtʲ]
stepmother	nevlastní matka (f)	[nɛvlastni: matka]
stepfather	nevlastní otec (m)	[nɛvlastni: otɛts]

infant	kojenec (m)	[kojenɛts]
baby (infant)	nemluvně (n)	[nɛmluvne]
little boy, kid	děcko (n)	[detsko]

wife	manželka (f)	[manʒelka]
husband	manžel (m)	[manʒel]
spouse (husband)	manžel (m)	[manʒel]
spouse (wife)	manželka (f)	[manʒelka]

married (masc.)	ženatý	[ʒenatɪ:]
married (fem.)	vdaná	[vdana:]
single (unmarried)	svobodný	[svobodnɪ:]
bachelor	mládenec (m)	[mla:dɛnɛts]
divorced (masc.)	rozvedený	[rozvɛdɛnɪ:]
widow	vdova (f)	[vdova]
widower	vdovec (m)	[vdovɛts]

relative	příbuzný (m)	[prʃi:buznɪ:]
close relative	blízký příbuzný (m)	[bli:zkɪ: prʃi:buznɪ:]
distant relative	vzdálený příbuzný (m)	[vzda:lɛnɪ: prʃi:buznɪ:]
relatives	příbuzenstvo (n)	[prʃi:buzɛnstvo]

orphan (boy or girl)	sirotek (m, f)	[sirotɛk]
guardian (of minor)	poručník (m)	[porutʃni:k]
to adopt (a boy)	adoptovat	[adoptovat]
to adopt (a girl)	adoptovat dívku	[adoptovat divku]

Medicine

47. Diseases

illness	nemoc (f)	[nɛmoʦ]
to be ill	být nemocný	[bɪːt nɛmoʦnɪː]
health	zdraví (n)	[zdrawiː]
runny nose (coryza)	rýma (f)	[rɪːma]
tonsillitis	angína (f)	[aɲiːna]
cold (illness)	nachlazení (n)	[naɦlazɛniː]
to catch a cold	nachladit se	[naɦladit sɛ]
bronchitis	bronchitida (f)	[bronɦitɪːda]
pneumonia	zápal (m) plic	[zaːpal pliʦ]
flu, influenza	chřipka (f)	[ɦr̝ʃipka]
short-sighted (adj)	krátkozraký	[kraːtkozrakɪː]
long-sighted (adj)	dalekozraký	[dalɛkozrakɪː]
squint	šilhavost (f)	[ʃilgavost]
squint-eyed (adj)	šilhavý	[ʃilgavɪː]
cataract	šedý zákal (m)	[ʃɛdɪː zaːkal]
glaucoma	zelený zákal (m)	[zɛlɛnɪː zaːkal]
stroke	mozková mrtvice (f)	[mozkova: mrtwiʦe]
heart attack	infarkt (m)	[infarkt]
myocardial infarction	infarkt (m) myokardu	[infarkt mijokardu]
paralysis	obrna (f)	[obrna]
to paralyse (vt)	paralyzovat	[paralizovat]
allergy	alergie (f)	[alɛrgie]
asthma	astma (n)	[astma]
diabetes	cukrovka (f)	[ʦukrovka]
toothache	bolení (n) zubů	[bolɛni: zubuː]
caries	zubní kaz (m)	[zubni: kaz]
diarrhoea	průjem (m)	[pruːjem]
constipation	zácpa (f)	[zaːʦpa]
stomach upset	žaludeční potíže (f pl)	[ʒaludɛʧni: poti:ʒe]
food poisoning	otrava (f)	[otrava]
to have a food poisoning	otrávit se	[otraːwit sɛ]
arthritis	artritida (f)	[artritɪːda]
rickets	rachitida (f)	[raɦitɪːda]
rheumatism	revmatismus (m)	[rɛvmatɪzmus]
atherosclerosis	ateroskleróza (f)	[atɛrosklɛroːza]
gastritis	gastritida (f)	[gastritɪːda]
appendicitis	apendicitida (f)	[apɛndiʦitɪːda]

| cholecystitis | zánět (m) žlučníku (m) | [za:net ʒlutʃni:ku] |
| ulcer | vřed (m) | [vrʒed] |

measles	spalničky (f pl)	[spalnitʃkɪ:]
German measles	zarděnky (f pl)	[zardeŋkɪ]
jaundice	žloutenka (f)	[ʒloutɛŋka]
hepatitis	hepatitida (f)	[gɛpatɪtɪ:da]

schizophrenia	schizofrenie (f)	[sɦizofrɛnɪje]
rabies (hydrophobia)	vzteklina (f)	[vstɛklina]
neurosis	neuróza (f)	[nɛuro:za]
concussion	otřes (m) mozku	[otrʃɛs mozku]

cancer	rakovina (f)	[rakowina]
sclerosis	skleróza (f)	[sklɛro:za]
multiple sclerosis	roztroušená skleróza (f)	[roztrouʃɛna: sklɛro:za]

alcoholism	alkoholismus (m)	[alkogolizmus]
alcoholic (n)	alkoholik (m)	[alkogolik]
syphilis	syfilida (f)	[sifili:da]
AIDS	AIDS (m)	[aidɛ:s]

tumour	nádor (m)	[na:dor]
malignant (adj)	zhoubný	[zgoubnɪ:]
benign (adj)	nezhoubný	[nɛzgoubnɪ:]

fever	zimnice (f)	[zimnitse]
malaria	malárie (f)	[mala:rije]
gangrene	gangréna (f)	[gaŋrɛ:na]
seasickness	mořská nemoc (f)	[morʃska: nɛmots]
epilepsy	padoucnice (f)	[padoutsnitse]

epidemic	epidemie (f)	[ɛpidɛmije]
typhus	tyf (m)	[tɪf]
tuberculosis	tuberkulóza (f)	[tubɛrkulo:za]
cholera	cholera (f)	[ɦolɛra]
plague (bubonic ~)	mor (m)	[mor]

48. Symptoms. Treatments. Part 1

symptom	příznak (m)	[prʃi:znak]
temperature	teplota (f)	[tɛplota]
fever	vysoká teplota (f)	[vɪsoka: tɛplota]
pulse	tep (m)	[tɛp]

giddiness	závrať (f)	[za:vratʲ]
hot (adj)	horký	[gorkɪ:]
shivering	mrazení (n)	[mrazɛni:]
pale (e.g. ~ face)	bledý	[blɛdɪ:]

cough	kašel (m)	[kaʃɛl]
to cough (vi)	kašlat	[kaʃlat]
to sneeze (vi)	kýchat	[kɪ:ɦat]
faint	mdloby (f pl)	[mdlobɪ]

to faint (vi)	upadnout do mdlob	[upadnout do mdlob]
bruise (hématome)	modřina (f)	[modrʒina]
bump (lump)	boule (f)	[boulɛ]
to bruise oneself	uhodit se	[ugodit sɛ]
bruise	pohmožděnina (f)	[pogmoʒdenina]
to get bruised	uhodit se	[ugodit sɛ]

to limp (vi)	kulhat	[kulgat]
dislocation	vykloubení (n)	[vɪkloubɛni:]
to dislocate (vt)	vykloubit	[vɪkloubit]
fracture	zlomenina (f)	[zlomɛnina]
to have a fracture	dostat zlomeninu	[dostat zlomɛninu]

cut (e.g. paper ~)	říznutí (n)	[rʒi:znuti:]
to cut oneself	říznout se	[rʒi:znout sɛ]
bleeding	krvácení (n)	[krva:tseni:]

| burn (injury) | popálenina (f) | [popa:lɛnina] |
| to burn oneself | spálit se | [spa:litsɛ] |

to prickle (vt)	píchnout	[pi:ɦnout]
to prickle oneself	píchnout se	[pi:ɦnout sɛ]
to injure (vt)	pohmoždit	[pogmoʒdit]
injury	pohmoždění (n)	[pogmoʒdeni:]
wound	rána (f)	[ra:na]
trauma	úraz (m)	[u:raz]

to be delirious	blouznit	[blouznit]
to stutter (vi)	zajíkat se	[zajɪ:kat sɛ]
sunstroke	úpal (m)	[u:pal]

49. Symptoms. Treatments. Part 2

| pain | bolest (f) | [bolɛst] |
| splinter (in foot, etc.) | tříska (f) | [trʃi:ska] |

sweat (perspiration)	pot (m)	[pot]
to sweat (perspire)	potit se	[potit sɛ]
vomiting	zvracení (n)	[zvratseni:]
convulsions	křeče (f pl)	[krʃɛtʃe]

pregnant (adj)	těhotná	[tegotna:]
to be born	narodit se	[narodit sɛ]
delivery, labour	porod (m)	[porod]
to labour (vi)	rodit	[rodit]
abortion	umělý potrat (m)	[umnelɪ: potrat]

respiration	dýchání (n)	[dɪ:ɦa:ni:]
inhalation	vdech (m)	[vdɛɦ]
exhalation	výdech (m)	[vɪ:dɛɦ]
to breathe out	vydechnout	[vɪdɛɦnout]
to breathe in	nadechnout se	[nadɛɦnout sɛ]
disabled person	invalida (m)	[invalida]
cripple	invalida (m)	[invalida]

drug addict	narkoman (m)	[narkoman]
deaf (adj)	hluchý	[gluɦɪ:]
dumb (adj)	němý	[nemɪ:]

mad, insane (adj)	šílený	[ʃi:lɛnɪ:]
madman	šílenec (m)	[ʃi:lɛnɛts]
madwoman	šílenec (f)	[ʃi:lɛnɛts]
to go insane	zešílet	[zɛʃi:lɛt]

gene	gen (m)	[gɛn]
immunity	imunita (f)	[imunita]
hereditary (adj)	dědičný	[dɛditʃnɪ:]
congenital (adj)	vrozený	[vrozɛnɪ:]

virus	virus (m)	[wirus]
microbe	mikrob (m)	[mikrob]
bacterium	baktérie (f)	[baktɛ:rije]
infection	infekce (f)	[infɛktse]

50. Symptoms. Treatments. Part 3

hospital	nemocnice (f)	[nɛmotsnitse]
patient	pacient (m)	[patsient]

diagnosis	diagnóza (f)	[dɪjagno:za]
cure	léčení (n)	[lɛ:tʃeni:]
medical treatment	léčení (n)	[lɛ:tʃeni:]
to get treatment	léčit se	[lɛ:tʃit sɛ]
to treat (vt)	ošetřovat	[oʃɛtrʃovat]
to nurse (look after)	ošetřovat	[oʃɛtrʃovat]
care	ošetřování (n)	[oʃɛtrʃova:ni:]

operation, surgery	operace (f)	[opɛratse]
to bandage (head, limb)	obvázat	[obva:zat]
bandaging	obvazování (n)	[obvazova:ni:]

vaccination	očkování (n)	[otʃkova:ni:]
to vaccinate (vt)	dělat očkování	[delat otʃkova:ni:]
injection, shot	injekce (f)	[inʰɛktse]
to give an injection	dávat injekci	[da:vat inʰɛktsi]

attack	záchvat (m)	[za:ɦvat]
amputation	amputace (f)	[amputatse]
to amputate (vt)	amputovat	[amputovat]
coma	kóma (n)	[ko:ma]
to be in a coma	být v kómatu	[bɛjt v ko:matu]
intensive care	reanimace (f)	[rɛanimatsɛ]

to recover (~ from flu)	uzdravovat se	[uzdravovat sɛ]
state (patient's ~)	stav (m)	[stav]
consciousness	vědomí (n)	[vʰedomi:]
memory (faculty)	paměť (f)	[pamneti]
to extract (tooth)	trhat	[trgat]
filling	plomba (f)	[plomba]

to fill (a tooth)	plombovat	[plombovat]
hypnosis	hypnóza (f)	[gipno:za]
to hypnotize (vt)	hypnotizovat	[gipnotɪzovat]

51. Doctors

doctor	lékař (m)	[lɛ:karʒ]
nurse	zdravotní sestra (f)	[zdravotni: sɛstra]
private physician	osobní lékař (m)	[osobni: lɛ:karʒ]

dentist	zubař (m)	[zubarʒ]
ophthalmologist	oční lékař (m)	[otʃni: lɛ:karʒ]
general practitioner	internista (m)	[intɛrnɪsta]
surgeon	chirurg (m)	[ɦirurg]

psychiatrist	psychiatr (m)	[psiɦijatr]
paediatrician	pediatr (m)	[pɛdɪjatr]
psychologist	psycholog (m)	[psiɦolog]
gynaecologist	gynekolog (m)	[ginɛkolog]
cardiologist	kardiolog (m)	[kardɪjolog]

52. Medicine. Drugs. Accessories

medicine, drug	lék (m)	[lɛ:k]
remedy	prostředek (m)	[prostrʃɛdɛk]
to prescribe (vt)	předepsat	[prʒɛdɛpsat]
prescription	recept (m)	[rɛtsept]

tablet, pill	tableta (f)	[tablɛta]
ointment	mast (f)	[mast]
ampoule	ampule (f)	[ampulɛ]
mixture	mixtura (f)	[mikstura]
syrup	sirup (m)	[sirup]
pill	pilulka (f)	[pilulka]
powder	prášek (m)	[pra:ʃɛk]

bandage	obvaz (m)	[obvaz]
cotton wool	vata (f)	[vata]
iodine	jód (m)	[jo:d]
plaster	leukoplast (m)	[lɛukoplast]
eyedropper	pipeta (f)	[pipɛta]
thermometer	teploměr (m)	[tɛplomner]
syringe	injekční stříkačka (f)	[inʰektʃni: strʃi:katʃka]

| wheelchair | vozík (m) | [vozi:k] |
| crutches | berle (f pl) | [bɛrlɛ] |

painkiller	anestetikum (n)	[anɛstɛtɪkum]
laxative	projímadlo (n)	[projɪ:madlo]
spirit (ethanol)	líh (m)	[li:ɦ]
medicinal herbs	bylina (f)	[bɪlina]
herbal (~ tea)	bylinný	[bɪlinɪ:]

HUMAN HABITAT

City

53. City. Life in the city

city, town	**město** (n)	[mnesto]
capital	**hlavní město** (n)	[glavni: mnesto]
village	**venkov** (m)	[vɛŋkov]
city map	**plán** (m) **města**	[pla:nɛk mnesta]
city centre	**střed** (m) **města**	[strʃɛd mnesta]
suburb	**předměstí** (n)	[prʃɛdmnesti:]
suburban (adj)	**předměstský**	[prʃɛdmnestski:]
outskirts	**okraj** (m)	[okraj]
environs (suburbs)	**okolí** (n)	[okoli:]
quarter	**čtvrt'** (f)	[tʃtvrtʲ]
residential quarter	**obytná čtvrt'** (f)	[obɪtna: tʃtvrtʲ]
traffic	**provoz** (m)	[provoz]
traffic lights	**semafor** (m)	[sɛmafor]
public transport	**městská doprava** (f)	[mnestska: doprava]
crossroads	**křižovatka** (f)	[krʃiʒovatka]
zebra crossing	**přechod** (m)	[prʃɛɦod]
pedestrian subway	**podchod** (m)	[podɦod]
to cross (vt)	**přecházet**	[prʃɛɦa:zɛt]
pedestrian	**chodec** (m)	[ɦodɛts]
pavement	**chodník** (m)	[ɦodni:k]
bridge	**most** (m)	[most]
embankment	**nábřeží** (n)	[na:brʒeʒi:]
fountain	**fontána** (f)	[fonta:na]
allée	**alej** (f)	[alɛj]
park	**park** (m)	[park]
boulevard	**bulvár** (m)	[bulva:r]
square	**náměstí** (n)	[na:mnesti:]
avenue (wide street)	**třída** (f)	[trʃi:da]
street	**ulice** (f)	[ulitse]
lane	**boční ulice** (f)	[botʃni: ulitse]
dead end	**slepá ulice** (f)	[slɛpa: ulitse]
house	**dům** (m)	[du:m]
building	**budova** (f)	[budova]
skyscraper	**mrakodrap** (m)	[mrakodrap]
facade	**fasáda** (f)	[fasa:da]
roof	**střecha** (f)	[strʃɛɦa]

window	okno (n)	[okno]
arch	oblouk (m)	[oblouk]
column	sloup (m)	[sloup]
corner	roh (m)	[roɦ]

shop window	výloha (f)	[vɪːloga]
shop sign	vývěsní tabule (f)	[vɪːwesni: tabulɛ]
poster	plakát (m)	[plakaːt]
advertising poster	reklamní plakát (m)	[rɛklamni: plakaːt]
hoarding	billboard (m)	[bilboːrd]

rubbish	odpadky (m pl)	[odpadkiː]
rubbish bin	popelnice (f)	[popɛlnitse]
to litter (vi)	dělat smetí	[delat smɛtiː]
rubbish dump	smetiště (n)	[smɛtiʃte]

telephone box	telefonní budka (f)	[tɛlɛfoni: budka]
street light	stožár (m) pouliční svítilny	[stoʒaːr pouliʧni: lampɪ]
bench (park ~)	lavička (f)	[lawiʧka]

policeman	policista (m)	[politsista]
police	policie (f)	[politsije]
beggar	žebrák (m)	[ʒebraːk]
homeless	bezdomovec (m)	[bɛzdomovɛts]

54. Urban institutions

shop	obchod (m)	[obɦod]
chemist, pharmacy	lékárna (f)	[lɛːkaːrna]
optician	oční optika (f)	[oʧni: optɪka]
shopping centre	obchodní středisko (n)	[obɦodni: strʃɛdisko]
supermarket	supermarket (m)	[supɛrmarket]

bakery	pekařství (n)	[pɛkarʃstwiː]
baker	pekař (m)	[pɛkarʒ]
cake shop	cukrárna (f)	[tsukraːrna]
grocery shop	smíšené zboží (n)	[smiʃɛnɛ zboʒiː]
butcher shop	řeznictví (n)	[rʒeznitstwiː]

greengrocer	zelinářství (n)	[zɛlinaːrʃstwiː]
market	tržnice (f)	[trʒnitsɛ]

coffee bar	kavárna (f)	[kavaːrna]
restaurant	restaurace (f)	[rɛstauratse]
pub	pivnice (f)	[pivnitse]
pizzeria	pizzerie (f)	[pitserie]

hairdresser	holičství (n) a kadeřnictví (n)	[goliʧstwi: a kadɛrʒnitstwiː]
post office	pošta (f)	[poʃta]
dry cleaners	čistírna (f)	[ʧisti:rna]
photo studio	fotografický ateliér (m)	[fotografitskɪ: atɛlijeːr]

shoe shop	obchod (m) s obuví	[obɦod s obuwi]
bookshop	knihkupectví (n)	[kniɦkupɛtstwiː]

sports shop	sportovní potřeby (f pl)	[sportovni: potrʃɛbɪ]
clothing repair	opravna (f) oděvů	[opravna odevu:]
formal wear hire	půjčovna (f) oděvů	[pu:jtʃovna odevu:]
DVD rental shop	půjčovna (f) filmů	[pu:jtʃovna filmu:]

circus	cirkus (m)	[tsirkus]
zoo	zoologická zahrada (f)	[zo:logɪtska: zagrada]
cinema	biograf (m)	[bijograf]
museum	muzeum (n)	[muzɛum]
library	knihovna (f)	[knigovna]

theatre	divadlo (n)	[divadlo]
opera	opera (f)	[opɛra]
nightclub	noční klub (m)	[notʃni: klub]
casino	kasino (n)	[kasi:no]

mosque	mešita (f)	[mɛʃita]
synagogue	synagóga (f)	[sinago:ga]
cathedral	katedrála (f)	[katɛdra:la]
temple	chrám (m)	[ɦra:m]
church	kostel (m)	[kostɛl]

institute	vysoká škola (f)	[vɪsoka: ʃkola]
university	univerzita (f)	[unɪvɛrzita]
school	škola (f)	[ʃkola]

prefecture	prefektura (f)	[prɛfɛktura]
town hall	magistrát (m)	[magistra:t]
hotel	hotel (m)	[gotɛl]
bank	banka (f)	[baŋka]

embassy	velvyslanectví (n)	[vɛlvɪslanɛtstwi:]
travel agency	cestovní kancelář (f)	[tsestovni: kantsela:rʒ]
information office	informační kancelář (f)	[informatʃni: kantsela:rʒ]
money exchange	směnárna (f)	[smnena:rna]

| underground, tube | metro (n) | [mɛtro] |
| hospital | nemocnice (f) | [nɛmotsnitse] |

| petrol station | benzínová pumpa (f) | [bɛnzi:nova: pumpa] |
| car park | parkoviště (n) | [parkowiʃte] |

55. Signs

shop sign	ukazatel (m) směru	[ukazatɛl smneru]
notice (written text)	nápis (m)	[na:pis]
poster	plakát (m)	[plaka:t]
direction sign	ukazatel (m)	[ukazatɛl]
arrow (sign)	šípka (f)	[ʃi:pka]

caution	varování (n)	[varova:ni:]
warning sign	výstraha (f)	[vɪ:straga]
to warn (vt)	upozorňovat	[upozorɲɔvat]
closing day	volný den (m)	[volnɪ dɛn]

| timetable (schedule) | jízdní řád (m) | [jıːzdni: rʒaːd] |
| opening hours | pracovní doba (f) | [pratsovni: doba] |

WELCOME!	VÍTEJTE!	[wiːtɛjtɛ]
ENTRANCE	VCHOD	[vɦod]
WAY OUT	VÝCHOD	[vɪːɦod]

PUSH	TAM	[tam]
PULL	SEM	[sɛm]
OPEN	OTEVŘENO	[otɛvrʒeno]
CLOSED	ZAVŘENO	[zavrʒeno]

| WOMEN | ŽENY | [ʒenı] |
| MEN | MUŽI | [muʒi] |

DISCOUNTS	SLEVY	[slɛvı]
SALE	VÝPRODEJ	[vɪːprodɛj]
NEW!	NOVINKA!	[nowiŋka]
FREE	ZDARMA	[zdarma]

ATTENTION!	POZOR!	[pozor]
NO VACANCIES	VOLNÁ MÍSTA NEJSOU	[volnaː miːsta nɛjsou]
RESERVED	ZADÁNO	[zadaːno]

| ADMINISTRATION | KANCELÁŘ | [kantsela:rʒ] |
| STAFF ONLY | POUZE PRO PERSONÁL | [pouzɛ pro personal] |

BEWARE OF THE DOG!	POZOR! ZLÝ PES	[pozor zlıː pɛs]
NO SMOKING	ZÁKAZ KOUŘENÍ	[zaːkaz kourʒeni:]
DO NOT TOUCH!	NEDOTÝKEJTE SE!	[nɛdotıːkɛjtɛ sɛ]

DANGEROUS	NEBEZPEČNÉ	[nɛbɛzpɛtʃnɛː]
DANGER	NEBEZPEČÍ	[nɛbɛzpɛtʃiː]
HIGH TENSION	VYSOKÉ NAPĚTÍ	[vɪsokɛ: napʰeti:]
NO SWIMMING!	KOUPÁNÍ ZAKÁZÁNO	[koupani: zaka:za:no]
OUT OF ORDER	MIMO PROVOZ	[mimo provoz]

FLAMMABLE	VYSOCE HOŘLAVÝ	[wisotsɛ ɦoʒlawi]
FORBIDDEN	ZAKAZ	[zaka:z]
NO TRESPASSING!	PRŮCHOD ZAKÁZÁN	[pruːɦod zaka:za:n]
WET PAINT	ČERSTVĚ NATŘENO	[tʃerstwe natʃeno]

56. Urban transport

bus, coach	autobus (m)	[autobus]
tram	tramvaj (f)	[tramvaj]
trolleybus	trolejbus (m)	[trolɛjbus]
route (of bus)	trasa (f)	[trasa]
number (e.g. bus ~)	číslo (n)	[tʃiː:slo]

to go by ...	jet	[jet]
to get on (~ the bus)	nastoupit do ...	[nastoupit do]
to get off ...	vystoupit z ...	[vıstoupit s]
stop (e.g. bus ~)	zastávka (f)	[zasta:vka]

next stop	příští zastávka (f)	[prʃiːʃti: zastaːvka]
terminus	konečná stanice (f)	[konɛtʃna: staniʦɛ]
timetable	jízdní řád (m)	[jɪːzdni: rʒaːd]
to wait (vt)	čekat	[tʃekat]

| ticket | jízdenka (f) | [jɪːzdɛŋka] |
| fare | jízdné (n) | [jɪːzdnɛː] |

cashier	pokladník (m)	[pokladniːk]
ticket inspection	kontrola (f)	[kontrola]
inspector	revizor (m)	[rɛwizor]

to be late (for ...)	mít zpoždění	[miːt spoʒdɛni]
to miss (~ the train, etc.)	opozdit se	[opozdit sɛ]
to be in a hurry	pospíchat	[pospiːɦat]

taxi, cab	taxík (m)	[taksiːk]
taxi driver	taxikář (m)	[taksikaːrʒ]
by taxi	taxíkem	[taksiːkɛm]
taxi rank	stanoviště (n) taxíků	[stanowiʃte taksiːkuː]
to call a taxi	zavolat taxíka	[zavolat taksiːka]
to take a taxi	vzít taxíka	[vziːt taksiːka]

traffic	uliční provoz (m)	[ulitʃni: provoz]
traffic jam	zácpa (f)	[zaːʦpa]
rush hour	špička (f)	[ʃpitʃka]
to park (vi)	parkovat se	[parkovat sɛ]
to park (vt)	parkovat	[parkovat]
car park	parkoviště (n)	[parkowiʃte]

underground, tube	metro (n)	[mɛtro]
station	stanice (f)	[stanitse]
to take the tube	jet metrem	[jet mɛtrɛm]
train	vlak (m)	[vlak]
train station	nádraží (n)	[naːdraʒi:]

57. Sightseeing

monument	památka (f)	[pamaːtka]
fortress	pevnost (f)	[pɛvnost]
palace	palác (m)	[palaːts]
castle	zámek (m)	[zaːmɛk]
tower	věž (f)	[vʰeʒ]
mausoleum	mauzoleum (n)	[mauzolɛum]

architecture	architektura (f)	[arɦitɛktura]
medieval (adj)	středověký	[strʃɛdovʰeki:]
ancient (adj)	starobylý	[starobɪlɪ:]
national (adj)	národní	[naːrodni:]
well-known (adj)	známý	[znaːmɪ:]

tourist	turista (m)	[turista]
guide (person)	průvodce (m)	[pruːvodʦɛ]
excursion	výlet (m)	[vɪːlɛt]

| to show (vt) | ukazovat | [ukazovat] |
| to tell (vt) | povídat | [powi:dat] |

to find (vt)	najít	[najı:t]
to get lost	ztratit se	[stratıtsɛ]
map (e.g. underground ~)	plán (m)	[pla:n]
map (e.g. city ~)	plán (m)	[pla:n]

souvenir, gift	suvenýr (m)	[suvɛnı:r]
gift shop	prodejna (f) suvenýrů	[prodɛjna suvɛnı:ru:]
to take pictures	fotografovat	[fotografovat]
to be photographed	fotografovat se	[fotografovat sɛ]

58. Shopping

to buy (purchase)	kupovat	[kupovat]
purchase	nákup (m)	[na:kup]
to go shopping	dělat nákupy	[delat na:kupı]
shopping	nakupování (n)	[nakupova:ni:]

| to be open (ab. shop) | být otevřen | [bı:t otɛvrʒen] |
| to be closed | být zavřen | [bı:t zavrʒen] |

footwear	obuv (f)	[obuv]
clothes, clothing	oblečení (n)	[oblɛtʃeni:]
cosmetics	kosmetika (f)	[kosmɛtıka]
food products	potraviny (f pl)	[potrawını]
gift, present	dárek (m)	[da:rɛk]

| shop assistant (masc.) | prodavač (m) | [prodavatʃ] |
| shop assistant (fem.) | prodavačka (f) | [prodavatʃka] |

cash desk	pokladna (f)	[pokladna]
mirror	zrcadlo (n)	[zrtsadlo]
counter (in shop)	pult (m)	[pult]
fitting room	zkušební kabinka (f)	[skuʃɛbni: kabiŋka]

to try on	zkusit	[skusit]
to fit (ab. dress, etc.)	hodit se	[godit sɛ]
to fancy (vt)	líbit se	[li:bit sɛ]

price	cena (f)	[tsena]
price tag	cenovka (f)	[tsenovka]
to cost (vt)	stát	[sta:t]
How much?	Kolik?	[kolik]
discount	sleva (f)	[slɛva]

inexpensive (adj)	levný	[lɛvnı:]
cheap (adj)	levný	[lɛvnı:]
expensive (adj)	drahý	[dragı:]
It's expensive	To je drahé	[to je dragɛ:]

| hire (n) | půjčování (n) | [pu:jtʃova:ni:] |
| to hire (~ a dinner jacket) | vypůjčit si | [vıpu:jtʃit si] |

| credit | úvěr (m) | [u:vʰer] |
| on credit (adv) | na splátky | [na spla:tki] |

59. Money

money	peníze (m pl)	[pɛni:zɛ]
exchange	výměna (f)	[vɪ:mnena]
exchange rate	kurz (m)	[kurz]
cashpoint	bankomat (m)	[baŋkomat]
coin	mince (f)	[mintse]

| dollar | dolar (m) | [dolar] |
| euro | euro (n) | [ɛuro] |

lira	lira (f)	[lira]
Deutschmark	marka (f)	[marka]
franc	frank (m)	[fraŋk]
pound sterling	libra (f) šterlinků	[libra ʃtɛrliŋku:]
yen	jen (m)	[jen]

debt	dluh (m)	[dluɦ]
debtor	dlužník (m)	[dluʒni:k]
to lend (money)	půjčit	[pu:jtʃit]
to borrow (vi, vt)	půjčit si	[pu:jtʃitsi]

bank	banka (f)	[baŋka]
account	účet (m)	[u:tʃet]
to deposit into the account	uložit na účet	[uloʒit na u:tʃet]
to withdraw (vt)	vybrat z účtu	[vɪbrat s u:tʃtu]

credit card	kreditní karta (f)	[krɛditni: karta]
cash	hotové peníze (m pl)	[gotovɛ: pɛni:zɛ]
cheque	šek (m)	[ʃɛk]
to write a cheque	vystavit šek	[vɪstawit ʃɛk]
chequebook	šeková knížka (f)	[ʃɛkova: kni:ʃka]

wallet	náprsní taška (f)	[na:prsni: taʃka]
purse	peněženka (f)	[pɛneʒeŋka]
billfold	portmonka (f)	[portmoŋka]
safe	trezor (m)	[trɛzor]

heir	dědic (m)	[dedits]
inheritance	dědictví (n)	[deditstwi:]
fortune (wealth)	majetek (m)	[majetɛk]

lease, let	nájem (m)	[na:jem]
rent money	činže (f)	[tʃinʒe]
to rent (sth from sb)	pronajímat si	[pronajɪ:mat si]

price	cena (f)	[tsena]
cost	cena (f)	[tsena]
sum	částka (f)	[tʃa:stka]
to spend (vt)	utrácet	[utra:tset]
expenses	náklady (m pl)	[na:kladɪ]

to economize (vi, vt)	šetřit	[ʃetrʃit]
thrifty (adj)	úsporný	[u:spornɪ:]
to pay (vi, vt)	platit	[platit]
payment	platba (f)	[platba]
change (give the ~)	peníze (m pl) nazpět	[pɛni:zɛ naspʰet]
tax	daň (f)	[daɲ]
fine	pokuta (f)	[pokuta]
to fine (vt)	pokutovat	[pokutovat]

60. Post. Postal service

post office	pošta (f)	[poʃta]
post (letters, etc.)	pošta (f)	[poʃta]
postman	listonoš (m)	[listonoʃ]
opening hours	pracovní doba (f)	[pratsovni: doba]
letter	dopis (m)	[dopis]
registered letter	doporučený dopis (m)	[doporutʃenɪ: dopis]
postcard	pohlednice (f)	[poglɛdnitse]
telegram	telegram (m)	[tɛlɛgram]
parcel	balík (m)	[bali:k]
money transfer	peněžní poukázka (f)	[pɛneʒni: pouka:zka]
to receive (vt)	dostat	[dostat]
to send (vt)	odeslat	[odɛslat]
sending	odeslání (n)	[odɛsla:ni:]
address	adresa (f)	[adrɛsa]
postcode	poštovní směrovací číslo (n)	[poʃtovni: smnerovatsi: tʃi:slo]
sender	odesílatel (m)	[odɛsi:latɛl]
receiver, addressee	příjemce (m)	[prʃi:jemtse]
name	jméno (n)	[jmɛ:no]
family name	příjmení (n)	[prʃi:jmɛni:]
rate (of postage)	tarif (m)	[tarif]
standard (adj)	normální	[norma:lni:]
economical (adj)	zlevněný	[zlɛvnenɪ:]
weight	váha (f)	[va:ga]
to weigh up (vt)	vážit	[va:ʒit]
envelope	obálka (f)	[oba:lka]
postage stamp	známka (f)	[zna:mka]
to stamp an envelope	nalepovat známku	[nalɛpovat zna:mku]

Dwelling. House. Home

61. House. Electricity

electricity	elektřina (f)	[ɛlɛktrʃina]
light bulb	žárovka (f)	[ʒaːrovka]
switch	vypínač (m)	[vɪpiːnaʧ]
fuse	pojistka (f)	[pojɪstka]
cable, wire (electric ~)	vodič (m)	[vodiʧ]
wiring	vedení (n)	[vɛdɛniː]
electricity meter	elektroměr (m)	[ɛlɛktromner]
readings	údaj (m)	[uːdaj]

62. Villa. Mansion

country house	venkovský dům (m)	[vɛŋkovskɪ duːm]
villa (by sea)	vila (f)	[wila]
wing (of building)	křídlo (n)	[krʃiːdlo]
garden	zahrada (f)	[zagrada]
park	park (m)	[park]
tropical glasshouse	oranžérie (f)	[oranʒeːrije]
to look after (garden, etc.)	zahradničit	[zagradniʧit]
swimming pool	bazén (m)	[bazɛːn]
gym	tělocvična (f)	[telotswiʧna]
tennis court	tenisový kurt (m)	[tɛnisovɪ kurt]
home cinema room	biograf (m)	[bijograf]
garage	garáž (f)	[garaːʒ]
private property	soukromé vlastnictví (n)	[soukromɛ vlastniʦtwiː]
private land	soukromý pozemek (m)	[soukromɪ pozɛmɛk]
warning (caution)	výstraha (f)	[vɪːstraga]
warning sign	výstražný nápis (m)	[vɪːstraʒnɪ naːpis]
security	stráž (f)	[straːʒ]
security guard	strážce (m)	[straːʒʦe]
burglar alarm	signalizace (f)	[signalizaʦe]

63. Flat

flat	byt (m)	[bɪt]
room	pokoj (m)	[pokoj]
bedroom	ložnice (f)	[loʒniʦe]

dining room	jídelna (f)	[jiːdɛlna]
living room	přijímací pokoj (m)	[prʃiˌjiːmaˌtsi: pokoj]
study	pracovna (f)	[pratsovna]

entry room	předsíň (f)	[prʃɛdsiːɲ]
bathroom	koupelna (f)	[koupɛlna]
water closet	záchod (m)	[zaːɦod]

ceiling	strop (m)	[strop]
floor	podlaha (f)	[podlaga]
corner	kout (m)	[kout]

64. Furniture. Interior

furniture	nábytek (m)	[naːbɪtɛk]
table	stůl (m)	[stuːl]
chair	židle (f)	[ʒidlɛ]
bed	lůžko (n)	[luːʒko]
sofa, settee	pohovka (f)	[pogovka]
armchair	křeslo (n)	[krʃɛslo]

bookcase	knihovna (f)	[knigovna]
shelf	police (f)	[politse]
set of shelves	etažér (m)	[ɛtaʒeːr]

wardrobe	skříň (f)	[skrʃiːɲ]
coat rack	věšák (m)	[vʰeʃaːk]
coat stand	věšák (m)	[vʰeʃaːk]

| chest of drawers | prádelník (m) | [praːdɛlniːk] |
| coffee table | konferenční stolek (m) | [konfɛrɛntʃniː stolɛk] |

mirror	zrcadlo (n)	[zrtsadlo]
carpet	koberec (m)	[kobɛrɛts]
small carpet	kobereček (m)	[kobɛrɛtʃek]

fireplace	krb (m)	[krb]
candle	svíce (f)	[swiːtse]
candlestick	svícen (m)	[swiːtsen]

drapes	záclony (f pl)	[zaːtslonɪ]
wallpaper	tapety (f pl)	[tapɛtɪ]
blinds (jalousie)	žaluzie (f)	[ʒaluzije]

| table lamp | stolní lampa (f) | [stolniː lampa] |
| wall lamp | svítidlo (n) | [swiːtidlo] |

| standard lamp | stojací lampa (f) | [stojatsiː lampa] |
| chandelier | lustr (m) | [lustr] |

leg (of chair, table)	noha (f)	[noga]
armrest	područka (f)	[podrutʃka]
back	opěradlo (n)	[opʰeradlo]
drawer	zásuvka (f)	[zaːsuvka]

65. Bedding

bedclothes	ložní prádlo (n)	[loʒni: pra:dlo]
pillow	polštář (m)	[polʃta:rʒ]
pillowslip	povlak (m) na polštář	[povlak na polʃta:rʒ]
blanket (eiderdown)	deka (f)	[dɛka]
sheet	prostěradlo (n)	[prosteradlo]
bedspread	přikrývka (f)	[prʃikrɪ:vka]

66. Kitchen

kitchen	kuchyně (f)	[kuɦɪne]
gas	plyn (m)	[plɪn]
gas cooker	plynový sporák (m)	[plɪnovɪ: spora:k]
electric cooker	elektrický sporák (m)	[ɛlɛktritskɪ: spora:k]
oven	trouba (f)	[trouba]
microwave oven	mikrovlnná pec (f)	[mikrovlna: pɛts]
refrigerator	lednička (f)	[lɛdnitʃka]
freezer	mrazicí komora (f)	[mrazitsi: komora]
dishwasher	myčka (f) nádobí	[mɪtʃka na:dobi:]
mincer	mlýnek (m) na maso	[mlɪ:nɛk na maso]
juicer	odšťavňovač (m)	[odʃtʲavnʒvatʃ]
toaster	opékač (m) topinek	[opɛ:katʃ topinɛk]
mixer	mixér (m)	[miksɛ:r]
coffee maker	kávovar (m)	[ka:vovar]
coffee pot	konvice (f) na kávu	[konwitse na ka:vu]
coffee grinder	mlýnek (m) na kávu	[mlɪ:nɛk na ka:vu]
kettle	čajník (m)	[tʃajni:k]
teapot	čajová konvice (f)	[tʃajova: konwitse]
lid	poklička (f)	[poklitʃka]
tea strainer	cedítko (n)	[tsedi:tko]
spoon	lžíce (f)	[lʒi:tse]
teaspoon	kávová lžička (f)	[ka:vova: lʒitʃka]
tablespoon	polévková lžíce (f)	[polɛːvkova: lʒi:tse]
fork	vidlička (f)	[widlitʃka]
knife	nůž (m)	[nu:ʒ]
tableware	nádobí (n)	[na:dobi:]
plate (dinner ~)	talíř (m)	[tali:rʒ]
saucer	talířek (m)	[tali:rʒek]
shot glass	sklenička (f)	[sklɛnitʃka]
glass (~ of water)	sklenice (f)	[sklɛnitse]
cup	šálek (m)	[ʃa:lɛk]
sugar bowl	cukřenka (f)	[tsukrʃɛŋka]
salt shaker	solnička (f)	[solnitʃka]
pepper shaker	pepřenka (f)	[pɛprʃɛŋka]

butter dish	nádobka (f) na máslo	[na:dobka na ma:slo]
stew pot	hrnec (m)	[grnɛts]
frying pan	pánev (f)	[pa:nɛv]
ladle	naběračka (f)	[nabʰeratʃka]
colander	cedník (m)	[tsedni:k]
tray	podnos (m)	[podnos]

bottle	láhev (f)	[la:gɛv]
jar (glass)	sklenice (f)	[sklɛnitse]
tin, can	plechovka (f)	[plɛɦovka]

bottle opener	otvírač (m) lahví	[otwi:ratʃ lagwi:]
tin opener	otvírač (m) konzerv	[otwi:ratʃ konzɛrv]
corkscrew	vývrtka (f)	[vı:vrtka]
filter	filtr (m)	[filtr]
to filter (vt)	filtrovat	[filtrovat]

| rubbish, refuse | odpadky (m pl) | [odpadki:] |
| rubbish bin | kbelík (m) na odpadky | [gbɛli:k na odpadkı] |

67. Bathroom

bathroom	koupelna (f)	[koupɛlna]
water	voda (f)	[voda]
tap	kohout (m)	[kogout]
hot water	teplá voda (f)	[tɛpla: voda]
cold water	studená voda (f)	[studɛna: voda]

| toothpaste | zubní pasta (f) | [zubni: pasta] |
| to clean one's teeth | čistit si zuby | [tʃistit si zubı] |

to shave (vi)	holit se	[golit sɛ]
shaving foam	pěna (f) na holení	[pʰena na golɛni:]
razor	holicí strojek (m)	[golitsi: strojek]

to wash (clean)	mýt	[mı:t]
to have a bath	mýt se	[mı:t sɛ]
shower	sprcha (f)	[sprɦa]
to have a shower	sprchovat se	[sprɦovat sɛ]

bath (tub)	vana (f)	[vana]
toilet	záchodová mísa (f)	[za:ɦodova: mi:sa]
sink (washbasin)	umývadlo (n)	[umı:vadlo]

| soap | mýdlo (m) | [mı:dlo] |
| soap dish | miska (f) na mýdlo | [miska na mı:dlo] |

sponge	mycí houba (f)	[mıtsi: gouba]
shampoo	šampon (m)	[ʃampon]
towel	ručník (m)	[rutʃni:k]
bathrobe	župan (m)	[ʒupan]

| laundry (process) | praní (n) | [prani:] |
| washing machine | pračka (f) | [pratʃka] |

| to do the laundry | prát | [pra:t] |
| washing powder | prací prášek (m) | [pratsi: pra:ʃɛk] |

68. Household appliances

TV, telly	televizor (m)	[tɛlɛwizor]
tape recorder	magnetofon (m)	[magnɛtofon]
video	videomagnetofon (m)	[widɛomagnɛtofon]
radio	přijímač (m)	[prʃijɪ:matʃ]
player (CD, MP3, etc.)	přehrávač (m)	[prʃɛgra:vatʃ]

video projector	projektor (m)	[projɛktor]
home cinema	domácí biograf (m)	[doma:tsi: bijograf]
DVD player	DVD přehrávač (m)	[dɛvɛdɛ prʃɛgra:vatʃ]
amplifier	zesilovač (m)	[zɛsilovatʃ]
video game console	hrací přístroj (m)	[gratsi: prʃi:stroj]

video camera	videokamera (f)	[widɛokamɛra]
camera (photo)	fotoaparát (m)	[fotoapara:t]
digital camera	digitální fotoaparát (m)	[digita:lni: fotoapara:t]

vacuum cleaner	vysavač (m)	[vɪsavatʃ]
iron (e.g. steam ~)	žehlička (f)	[ʒeglitʃka]
ironing board	žehlicí prkno (n)	[ʒeglitsi: prkno]

telephone	telefon (m)	[tɛlɛfon]
mobile phone	mobilní telefon (m)	[mobilni: tɛlɛfon]
typewriter	psací stroj (m)	[psatsi: stroj]
sewing machine	šicí stroj (m)	[ʃitsi: stroj]

microphone	mikrofon (m)	[mikrofon]
headphones	sluchátka (n pl)	[sluɦa:tka]
remote control (TV)	ovládač (m)	[ovla:datʃ]

CD, compact disc	CD disk (m)	[tsedɛ dɪsk]
cassette	kazeta (f)	[kazɛta]
vinyl record	deska (f)	[dɛska]

Job. Business. Part 1

69. Office. Working in the office

office (of firm)	kancelář (f)	[kantsela:rʒ]
office (of director, etc.)	pracovna (f)	[pratsovna]
reception	recepce (f)	[rɛtseptse]
secretary	tajemník (m)	[tajemni:k]
director	ředitel (m)	[rʒeditɛl]
manager	manažer (m)	[manaʒer]
accountant	účetní (m, f)	[u:tʃetni:]
employee	zaměstnanec (m)	[zamnestnanɛts]
furniture	nábytek (m)	[na:bɪtɛk]
desk	stůl (m)	[stu:l]
desk chair	křeslo (n)	[krʃɛslo]
chest of drawers	skřínka (f)	[skrʃi:ɲka]
coat stand	věšák (m)	[vʰeʃa:k]
computer	počítač (m)	[potʃi:tatʃ]
printer	tiskárna (f)	[tiska:rna]
fax machine	fax (m)	[faks]
photocopier	kopírovací přístroj (m)	[kopi:rovatsi: prʃi:stroj]
paper	papír (m)	[papi:r]
office supplies	kancelářské potřeby (f pl)	[kantselarʃskɛ: potrʃɛbɪ]
mouse mat	podložka (f) pro myš	[podloʒka pro mɪʃ]
sheet of paper	list (m)	[list]
folder, binder	fascikl (m)	[fastsikl]
catalogue	katalog (m)	[katalog]
directory (of addresses)	příručka (f)	[prʃi:rutʃka]
documentation	dokumentace (f)	[dokumɛntatse]
brochure	brožura (f)	[broʒura]
leaflet	leták (m)	[lɛta:k]
sample	vzor (m)	[vzor]
training meeting	trénink (m)	[trɛ:nɪŋk]
meeting (of managers)	porada (f)	[porada]
lunch time	polední přestávka (f)	[polɛdni: prʃɛsta:vka]
to make a copy	dělat kopii	[delat kopijɪ]
to make copies	rozmnožit	[rozmnoʒit]
to receive a fax	přijímat fax	[prʃiji:mat faks]
to send a fax	odesílat fax	[odɛsi:lat faks]
to ring (telephone)	zavolat	[zavolat]
to answer (vt)	odpovědět	[odpovʰedet]
to put through	spojit	[spojɪ:t]

to arrange, to set up	stanovovat	[stanovovat]
to demonstrate (vt)	demonstrovat	[dɛmonstrovat]
to be absent	být nepřítomen	[bɪ:t nɛprʃi:tomɛn]
absence	absence (f)	[absɛntse]

70. Business processes. Part 1

occupation	práce (f)	[pra:tse]
firm	firma (f)	[firma]
company	společnost (f)	[spolɛtʃnost]
corporation	korporace (f)	[korporatse]
enterprise	podnik (m)	[podnik]
agency	agentura (f)	[agɛntura]

agreement (contract)	smlouva (f)	[smlouva]
contract	kontrakt (m)	[kontrakt]
deal	obchod (m)	[obɦod]
order (to place an ~)	objednávka (f)	[obʰedna:vka]
term (of contract)	podmínka (f)	[podmi:ŋka]

wholesale (adv)	ve velkém	[vɛ vɛlkɛ:m]
wholesale (adj)	velkoobchodní	[vɛlko:bɦodni:]
wholesale (n)	prodej (m) ve velkém	[prodɛj vɛ vɛlkɛ:m]
retail (adj)	maloobchodní	[malo:bɦodni:]
retail (n)	prodej (m) v drobném	[prodɛj v drobnɛ:m]

competitor	konkurent (m)	[koŋkurɛnt]
competition	konkurence (f)	[koŋkurɛntse]
to compete (vi)	konkurovat	[koŋkurovat]

| partner (associate) | partner (m) | [partnɛr] |
| partnership | partnerství (n) | [partnɛrstwi:] |

crisis	krize (f)	[krizɛ]
bankruptcy	bankrot (m)	[baŋkrot]
to go bankrupt	zbankrotovat	[zbaŋkrotovat]
difficulty	potíž (f)	[poti:ʒ]
problem	problém (m)	[problɛ:m]
catastrophe	katastrofa (f)	[katastrofa]

economy	ekonomika (f)	[ɛkonomika]
economic (~ growth)	ekonomický	[ɛkonomitskɪ:]
economic recession	hospodářský pokles (m)	[gospoda:rʃskɪ: poklɛs]

| goal (aim) | cíl (m) | [tsi:l] |
| task | úkol (m) | [u:kol] |

to trade (vi)	obchodovat	[obɦodovat]
network (distribution ~)	síť' (f)	[si:tʲ]
inventory (stock)	sklad (m)	[sklad]
assortment	sortiment (m)	[sortɪmɛnt]

| leader | předák (m) | [prʃɛda:k] |
| large (~ company) | velký | [vɛlkɪ:] |

monopoly	monopol (m)	[monopol]
theory	teorie (f)	[tɛorije]
practice	praxe (f)	[praksɛ]
experience (in my ~)	zkušenost (f)	[skuʃɛnost]
trend (tendency)	tendence (f)	[tɛndɛntsɛ]
development	rozvoj (m)	[rozvoj]

71. Business processes. Part 2

| profitability | výhoda (f) | [vɪːgoda] |
| profitable (adj) | výhodný | [vɪːgodnɪː] |

delegation (group)	delegace (f)	[dɛlɛgatsɛ]
salary	mzda (f)	[mzda]
to correct (an error)	opravovat	[opravovat]
business trip	služební cesta (f)	[sluʒebniː tsesta]
commission	komise (f)	[komisɛ]

to control (vt)	kontrolovat	[kontrolovat]
conference	konference (f)	[konfɛrɛntsɛ]
licence	licence (f)	[litsentsɛ]
reliable (~ partner)	spolehlivý	[spolɛglivɪː]

initiative	iniciativa (f)	[inɪtsijatɪva]
norm (standard)	norma (f)	[norma]
circumstance	okolnost (f)	[okolnost]
duty (of employee)	povinnost (f)	[powinost]

enterprise	organizace (f)	[organɪzatsɛ]
organization (process)	organizace (f)	[organɪzatsɛ]
organized (adj)	organizovaný	[organɪzovanɪː]
cancellation	zrušení (n)	[zruʃɛniː]
to cancel (call off)	zrušit	[zruʃit]
report (official ~)	zpráva (f)	[spraːva]

patent	patent (m)	[patɛnt]
to patent (obtain patent)	patentovat	[patɛntovat]
to plan (vt)	plánovat	[plaːnovat]

bonus (money)	prémie (f)	[prɛːmie]
professional (adj)	profesionální	[profɛsijonaːlniː]
procedure	procedura (f)	[protsedura]

to examine (contract, etc.)	projednat	[projednat]
calculation	výpočet (m)	[vɪːpotʃet]
reputation	reputace (f)	[rɛputatsɛ]
risk	riziko (n)	[riziko]

to manage, to run	řídit	[rʒiːdit]
information	údaje (m pl)	[uːdaje]
property	vlastnictví (n)	[vlastnitstwiː]
union	unie (f)	[unɪje]
life insurance	pojištění (n) života	[pojiʃteni ʒivota]
to insure (vt)	pojišťovat	[pojiʃtɜvat]

insurance	pojistka (f)	[pojɪstka]
auction	dražba (f)	[draʒba]
to notify (inform)	uvědomit	[uvʰedomit]
management (process)	řízení (n)	[rʒiːzɛniː]
service (~ industry)	služba (f)	[sluʒba]

forum	fórum (n)	[foːrum]
to function (vi)	fungovat	[fuŋovat]
stage (phase)	etapa (f)	[ɛtapa]
legal (~ services)	právnický	[praːvniʦkɪ]
lawyer (legal expert)	právník (m)	[praːvniːk]

72. Production. Works

plant	závod (m)	[zaːvod]
factory	továrna (f)	[tovaːrna]
workshop	dílna (f)	[diːlna]
production site	podnik (m)	[podnik]

industry	průmysl (m)	[pruːmɪsl]
industrial (adj)	průmyslový	[pruːmɪslovɪ]
heavy industry	těžký průmysl (m)	[teʒki pruːmɪsl]
light industry	lehký průmysl (m)	[lɛɦkɪ pruːmɪsl]

products	výroba (f)	[vɪːroba]
to produce (vt)	vyrábět	[vɪraːbʰet]
raw materials	surovina (f)	[surowina]

foreman	četař (m)	[ʧetarʒ]
workers team	brigáda (f)	[brigaːda]
worker	dělník (m)	[delniːk]

working day	pracovní den (m)	[praʦovniː dɛn]
pause	přestávka (f)	[prʃɛstaːvka]
meeting	schůze (f)	[sɦuːzɛ]
to discuss (vt)	projednávat	[projednaːvat]

plan	plán (m)	[plaːn]
to fulfil the plan	plnit plán	[plnit plaːn]
rate of output	norma (f)	[norma]
quality	kvalita (f)	[kvalita]
checking (control)	kontrola (f)	[kontrola]
quality control	kontrola (f) kvality	[kontrola kvalitɪ]

safety of work	bezpečnost (f) práce	[bɛzpɛʧnost praːʦe]
discipline	kázeň (f)	[kaːzɲ]
infringement	přestupek (m)	[prʃɛstupɛk]
to infringe (rules)	nedodržovat	[nɛdodrʒovat]

strike	stávka (f)	[staːvka]
striker	stávkující (m)	[staːvkujɪʦiː]
to be on strike	stávkovat	[staːvkovat]
trade union	odbory (m)	[odborɪ]
to invent (machine, etc.)	vynalézat	[vɪnalɛːzat]

invention	vynález (m)	[vɪnalɛ:z]
research	výzkum (m)	[vɪ:skum]
to improve (make better)	zlepšovat	[zlɛpʃovat]

| technology | technologie (f) | [tɛɦnologije] |
| technical drawing | výkres (m) | [vɪ:krɛs] |

load, cargo	náklad (m)	[na:klad]
loader (person)	nakládač (m)	[nakla:datʃ]
to load (vehicle, etc.)	nakládat	[nakla:dat]
loading (process)	nakládání (n)	[nakla:da:ni:]

| to unload (vi, vt) | vykládat | [vɪkla:dat] |
| unloading | vykládání (n) | [vɪkla:da:ni:] |

transport	doprava (f)	[doprava]
transport company	dopravní společnost (f)	[dopravni: spolɛtʃnost]
to transport (vt)	dopravovat	[dopravovat]

wagon	nákladní vůz (m)	[na:kladni: vu:z]
cistern	cisterna (f)	[tsɪstɛrna]
lorry	nákladní auto (n)	[na:kladni: auto]

| machine tool | stroj (m) | [stroj] |
| mechanism | mechanismus (m) | [mɛɦanɪzmus] |

industrial waste	odpad (m)	[odpad]
packing (process)	balení (n)	[balɛni:]
to pack (vt)	zabalit	[zabalit]

73. Contract. Agreement

contract	kontrakt (m)	[kontrakt]
agreement	dohoda (f)	[dogoda]
addendum	příloha (f)	[prʃi:loga]

to sign a contract	uzavřít kontrakt	[uzavrʒi:t kontrakt]
signature	podpis (m)	[podpis]
to sign (vt)	podepsat	[podɛpsat]
stamp (seal)	razítko (n)	[razi:tko]

| subject of contract | předmět (m) smlouvy | [prʃɛdmnet smlouvɪ] |
| clause | bod (m) | [bod] |

| parties (in contract) | strany (f pl) | [stranɪ] |
| legal address | sídlo (n) | [si:dlo] |

| to break the contract | porušit kontrakt | [poruʃit kontrakt] |
| commitment | závazek (m) | [za:vazɛk] |

responsibility	odpovědnost (f)	[odpovʰednost]
force majeure	vyšší moc (f)	[vɪʃi: mots]
dispute	spor (m)	[spor]
penalties	sankční pokuta (f)	[saŋktʃni: pokuta]

74. Import & Export

import	dovoz (m)	[dovoz]
importer	dovozce (m)	[dovoztse]
to import (vt)	dovážet	[dova:ʒet]
import (e.g. ~ goods)	z dovozu	[z dovozu]

exporter	vývozce (m)	[vɪ:voztse]
to export (vi, vt)	vyvážet	[vɪva:ʒet]

goods	zboží (n)	[zboʒi:]
consignment, lot	partie (f)	[partije]

weight	váha (f)	[va:ga]
volume	objem (m)	[obʰem]
cubic metre	krychlový metr (m)	[krɪɦlovɪ: mɛtr]

manufacturer	výrobce (m)	[vɪ:robtse]
transport company	dopravní společnost (f)	[dopravni: spolɛtʃnost]
container	kontejner (m)	[kontɛjnɛr]

border	hranice (f)	[granitse]
customs	celnice (f)	[tselnitse]
customs duty	clo (n)	[tslo]
customs officer	celník (m)	[tselni:k]
smuggling	pašování (n)	[paʃova:ni:]
contraband (goods)	pašované zboží (n pl)	[paʃovanɛ: zboʒi:]

75. Finances

share, stock	akcie (f)	[aktsije]
bond (certificate)	dluhopis (m)	[dlugopis]
bill of exchange	směnka (f)	[smneŋka]

stock exchange	burza (f)	[burza]
stock price	kurz (m) akcií	[kurs aktsijɪ:]

to become cheaper	zlevnět	[zlɛvnet]
to rise in price	zdražit	[zdraʒit]

share	podíl (m)	[podi:l]
controlling interest	kontrolní balík (m)	[kontrolni: bali:k]

investment	investice (f pl)	[invɛstɪtse]
to invest (vt)	investovat	[invɛstovat]
percent	procento (n)	[protsento]
interest (on investment)	úroky (m pl)	[u:rokɪ]

profit	zisk (m)	[zisk]
profitable (adj)	ziskový	[ziskovɪ:]
tax	daň (f)	[daɲ]
currency (foreign ~)	měna (f)	[mnena]
national (adj)	národní	[na:rodni:]

exchange (currency ~)	výměna (f)	[vɪ:mnena]
accountant	účetní (m, f)	[u:tʃetni:]
accounting	účtárna (f)	[u:tʃta:rna]

bankruptcy	bankrot (m)	[baŋkrot]
collapse, ruin	krach (m)	[kraɦ]
ruin	bankrot (m)	[baŋkrot]
to be ruined	zkrachovat	[skraɦovat]
inflation	inflace (f)	[inflatse]
devaluation	devalvace (f)	[dɛvalvatse]

capital	kapitál (m)	[kapita:l]
income	příjem (m)	[prʃi:jem]
turnover	obrat (m)	[obrat]
resources	zdroje (m pl)	[zdroje]
monetary resources	peněžní prostředky (m pl)	[pɛneʒni: prostrʃɛdkɪ]
to reduce (expenses)	snížit	[sni:ʒit]

76. Marketing

marketing	marketing (m)	[markɛtiŋ]
market	trh (m)	[trg]
market segment	segment (m) trhu	[sɛgmɛnt trgu]
product	produkt (m)	[produkt]
goods	zboží (n)	[zboʒi:]

brand	obchodní značka (f)	[obɦodni: znatʃka]
logotype	firemní značka (f)	[firɛmni: znatʃka]
logo	logo (n)	[logo]

demand	poptávka (f)	[popta:vka]
supply	nabídka (f)	[nabi:dka]
need	potřeba (f)	[potrʃɛba]
consumer	spotřebitel (m)	[spotrʃɛbitɛl]

analysis	analýza (f)	[anali:za]
to analyse (vt)	analyzovat	[analizovat]
positioning	určování (n) pozice	[urtʃova:ni: pozitse]
to position (vt)	určovat pozici	[urtʃovat pozitsi]

price	cena (f)	[tsena]
pricing policy	cenová politika (f)	[tsenova: politika]
pricing	tvorba (f) cen	[tvorba tsen]

77. Advertising

advertising	reklama (f)	[rɛklama]
to advertise (vt)	dělat reklamu	[delat rɛklamu]
budget	rozpočet (m)	[rozpotʃet]

| ad, advertisement | reklama (f) | [rɛklama] |
| TV advertising | televizní reklama (f) | [tɛlɛwizni: rɛklama] |

| radio advertising | rozhlasová reklama (f) | [rozglasova: rɛklama] |
| outdoor advertising | venkovní reklama (f) | [vɛŋkovni: rɛklama] |

mass medias	média (n pl)	[mɛ:dɪja]
periodical (n)	periodikum (n)	[pɛrijodɪkum]
image (public appearance)	image (f)	[imiʤ]

| slogan | heslo (n) | [gɛslo] |
| motto (maxim) | heslo (n) | [gɛslo] |

campaign	kampaň (f)	[kampaɲ]
advertising campaign	reklamní kampaň (f)	[rɛklamni: kampaɲ]
target group	cílové posluchačstvo (n)	[ʦi:lovɛ: posluɦaʧstvo]

business card	vizitka (f)	[wizitka]
leaflet	leták (m)	[lɛta:k]
brochure	brožura (f)	[broʒura]
pamphlet	skládanka (f)	[skla:daŋka]
newsletter	bulletin (m)	[biltɛ:n]

shop sign	reklamní tabule (f)	[rɛklamni: tabulɛ]
poster	plakát (m)	[plaka:t]
hoarding	billboard (m)	[bilbo:rd]

78. Banking

| bank | banka (f) | [baŋka] |
| branch (of bank, etc.) | pobočka (f) | [poboʧka] |

| consultant | konzultant (m) | [konzultant] |
| manager (director) | správce (m) | [spra:vʦe] |

bank account	·	účet (m)	[u:ʧet]
account number	číslo (n) účtu	[ʧi:slo u:ʧtu]
current account	běžný účet (m)	[bʰeʒnɪ: u:ʧet]
deposit account	spořitelní účet (m)	[sporʒitɛlni: u:ʧet]

to open an account	založit účet	[zaloʒit u:ʧet]
to close the account	uzavřít účet	[uzavrʒi:t u:ʧet]
to deposit into the account	uložit na účet	[uloʒit na u:ʧet]
to withdraw (vt)	vybrat z účtu	[vɪbrat s u:ʧtu]

deposit	vklad (m)	[vklad]
to make a deposit	uložit vklad	[uloʒit vklad]
wire transfer	převod (m)	[prʃɛvod]
to wire (money)	převést	[prʃɛvɛ:st]

| sum | částka (f) | [ʧa:stka] |
| How much? | Kolik? | [kolik] |

signature	podpis (m)	[podpis]
to sign (vt)	podepsat	[podɛpsat]
credit card	kreditní karta (f)	[krɛditni: karta]
code	kód (m)	[ko:d]

| credit card number | číslo (n) kreditní karty | [ʧi:slo krɛditni: kartı] |
| cashpoint | bankomat (m) | [baŋkomat] |

cheque	šek (m)	[ʃɛk]
to write a cheque	vystavit šek	[vıstawit ʃɛk]
chequebook	šeková knížka (f)	[ʃɛkova: kni:ʃka]

loan (bank ~)	úvěr (m)	[u:vʰer]
to apply for a loan	žádat o úvěr	[ʒa:dat o u:vʰer]
to get a loan	brát na úvěr	[bra:t na u:vʰer]
to give a loan	poskytovat úvěr	[poskıtovat u:vʰer]
guarantee	kauce (f)	[kauʦe]

79. Telephone. Phone conversation

telephone	telefon (m)	[tɛlɛfon]
mobile phone	mobilní telefon (m)	[mobilni: tɛlɛfon]
answering machine	záznamník (m)	[za:znamni:k]

| to ring (telephone) | volat | [volat] |
| call, ring | volání (n) | [vola:ni:] |

to dial a number	vytočit číslo	[vıtoʧit ʧi:slo]
Hello!	Prosím!	[prosi:m]
to ask (vt)	zeptat se	[zɛptat sɛ]
to answer (vi, vt)	odpovědět	[odpovʰedet]

to hear (vt)	slyšet	[slıʃɛt]
well (adv)	dobře	[dobrʒe]
not well (adv)	špatně	[ʃpatne]
noises (interference)	poruchy (f pl)	[poruɦı]

receiver	sluchátko (n)	[sluɦa:tko]
to pick up (~ the phone)	vzít sluchátko	[vzi:t sluɦa:tko]
to hang up (~ the phone)	zavěsit sluchátko	[zavʰesit sluɦa:tko]

engaged (adj)	obsazeno	[obsazɛno]
to ring (ab. phone)	zvonit	[zvonit]
telephone book	telefonní seznam (m)	[tɛlɛfoɲi: sɛznam]

local (adj)	místní	[mi:stni:]
trunk (e.g. ~ call)	dálkový	[daʎkowi]
international (adj)	mezinárodní	[mɛzina:rodni:]

80. Mobile telephone

mobile phone	mobilní telefon (m)	[mobilni: tɛlɛfon]
display	displej (m)	[dısplɛj]
button	tlačítko (n)	[tlaʧi:tko]
SIM card	SIM karta (f)	[sim karta]
battery	baterie (f)	[batɛrije]
to be flat (battery)	vybít se	[vıbi:t sɛ]

charger	nabíječka (f) baterií	[nabi:jetʃka batɛrijɪ:]
menu	nabídka (f)	[nabi:dka]
settings	nastavení (n)	[nastavɛni:]
tune (melody)	melodie (f)	[mɛlodɪje]
to select (vt)	vybrat	[vɪbrat]

calculator	kalkulačka (f)	[kalkulatʃka]
answering machine	záznamník (m)	[za:znamni:k]
alarm clock	budík (m)	[budi:k]
contacts	telefonní seznam (m)	[tɛlɛfoɲi: sɛznam]

| SMS (text message) | SMS zpráva (f) | [ɛsɛmɛs spra:va] |
| subscriber | účastník (m) | [u:tʃastni:k] |

81. Stationery

| ballpoint pen | pero (n) | [pɛro] |
| fountain pen | plnicí pero (n) | [plnitsi: pɛro] |

pencil	tužka (f)	[tuʃka]
highlighter	značkovač (m)	[znatʃkovatʃ]
felt-tip pen	fix (m)	[fiks]

| notepad | notes (m) | [notɛs] |
| diary | diář (m) | [dia:rʒ] |

ruler	pravítko (n)	[prawi:tko]
calculator	kalkulačka (f)	[kalkulatʃka]
rubber	guma (f)	[guma]
drawing pin	napínáček (m)	[napi:na:tʃek]
paper clip	svorka (f)	[svorka]

glue	lepidlo (n)	[lɛpidlo]
stapler	sešívačka (f)	[sɛʃi:vatʃka]
hole punch	dírkovačka (f)	[di:rkovatʃka]
pencil sharpener	ořezávátko (n)	[orʒeza:va:tko]

82. Kinds of business

accounting services	účetnické služby (f pl)	[u:tʃetnitskɛ: sluʒbɪ]
advertising	reklama (f)	[rɛklama]
advertising agency	reklamní agentura (f)	[rɛklamni: agɛntura]
air-conditioners	klimatizátory (m pl)	[klimatiza:torɪ]
airline	letecká společnost (f)	[lɛtɛtska: spolɛtʃnost]

alcoholic drinks	alkoholické nápoje (m pl)	[alkogolitskɛ: na:poje]
antiques	starožitnictví (n)	[staroʒitnitstwi:]
art gallery	galerie (f)	[galɛrije]
audit services	auditorské služby (f pl)	[auditorskɛ: sluʒbɪ]

| banks | bankovnictví (n) | [baŋkovnitstwi:] |
| beauty salon | kosmetický salón (m) | [kosmɛtitskɪ: salo:n] |

bookshop	knihkupectví (n)	[kniħkupɛtstwi:]
brewery	pivovar (m)	[pivovar]
business centre	obchodní centrum (n)	[obħodni: tsentrum]
business school	obchodní škola (f)	[obħodni: ʃkola]

casino	kasino (n)	[kasi:no]
chemist, pharmacy	lékárna (f)	[lɛ:ka:rna]
cinema	biograf (m)	[bijograf]
construction	stavebnictví (n)	[stavɛbnitstwi:]
consulting	poradenství (n)	[poradɛnstwi:]

dentistry	stomatologie (f)	[stomatologije]
design	design (m)	[dɪzajn]
dry cleaners	čistírna (f)	[tʃisti:rna]

employment agency	kádrová kancelář (f)	[ka:drova: kantsela:rʒ]
financial services	finanční služby (f pl)	[finantʃni: sluʒbɪ]
food products	potraviny (f pl)	[potrawinɪ]
furniture (for house)	nábytek (m)	[na:bɪtɛk]
garment	oblečení (n)	[oblɛtʃeni:]
hotel	hotel (m)	[gotɛl]

ice-cream	zmrzlina (f)	[zmrzlina]
industry	průmysl (m)	[pru:mɪsl]
insurance	pojištění (n)	[pojɪʃteni:]
Internet	internet (m)	[intɛrnɛt]
investment	investice (f pl)	[invɛstɪtse]
jeweller	klenotník (m)	[klɛnotni:k]
jewellery	klenotnické výrobky (m pl)	[klɛnotnitskɛ: vɪ:robkɪ]

laundry (room, shop)	prádelna (f)	[pra:dɛlna]
legal adviser	právnické služby (f pl)	[pra:vnitskɛ: sluʒbɪ]
light industry	lehký průmysl (m)	[lɛħkɪ: pru:mɪsl]

magazine	časopis (m)	[tʃasopis]
mail-order selling	prodej (m) podle katalogu	[prodɛj podlɛ katalogu]
medicine	lékařství (n)	[lɛ:karʃtwi:]
museum	muzeum (n)	[muzɛum]

news agency	zpravodajská agentura (f)	[spravodajska: agɛntura]
newspaper	noviny (f pl)	[nowinɪ]
nightclub	noční klub (m)	[notʃni: klub]

oil (petroleum)	ropa (f)	[ropa]
parcels service	kurýrská služba (f)	[kuri:rska: sluʒba]
pharmaceuticals	farmacie (f)	[farmatsije]
printing (industry)	polygrafie (f)	[poligrafije]
pub	bar (m)	[bar]
publishing house	nakladatelství (n)	[nakladatɛlstwi:]

radio	rozhlas (m)	[rozglas]
real estate	nemovitost (f)	[nɛmowitost]
restaurant	restaurace (f)	[rɛstauratse]

| security agency | bezpečnostní agentura (f) | [bɛzpɛtʃnostni: agɛntura] |
| shop | obchod (m) | [obħod] |

sport	sport (m)	[sport]
stock exchange	burza (f)	[burza]
supermarket	supermarket (m)	[supɛrmarket]
swimming pool	bazén (m)	[bazɛ:n]

tailors	módní salón (m)	[mo:dni: salo:n]
television	televize (f)	[tɛlɛwizɛ]
theatre	divadlo (n)	[divadlo]
trade	obchod (m)	[obɦod]
transport companies	přeprava (f)	[prʃɛprava]
travel	cestovní ruch (m)	[ʦestovni: ruɦ]

undertakers	pohřební ústav (m)	[pogrʒebni: u:stav]
veterinary surgeon	zvěrolékař (m)	[zvʰerolɛ:karʒ]
warehouse	sklad (m)	[sklad]
waste collection	vyvážení (n) odpadků	[vɪva:ʒeni: odpadku:]

HUMAN ACTIVITIES

Job. Business. Part 2

83. Show. Exhibition

exhibition, show	výstava (f)	[vɪːstava]
trade show	obchodní výstava (f)	[obɦodni: vɪːstava]
participation	účast (f)	[u:tʃast]
to participate (vi)	zúčastnit se	[zu:tʃastnit sɛ]
participant (exhibitor)	účastník (m)	[u:tʃastni:k]
director	ředitel (m)	[rʒeditɛl]
organizer's office	organizační výbor (m)	[organizatʃni: vɪːbor]
organizer	organizátor (m)	[organɪza:tor]
to organize (vt)	organizovat	[organɪzovat]
participation form	přihláška (f) k účasti	[prʃigla:ʃka k u:tʃasti]
to fill in (vt)	vyplnit	[vɪplnit]
details	podrobnosti (f pl)	[podrobnosti]
information	informace (f)	[informatse]
price	cena (f)	[tsena]
including	včetně	[vtʃetne]
to include (vt)	zahrnovat	[zagrnovat]
to pay (vi, vt)	platit	[platit]
registration fee	registrační poplatek (m)	[rɛgistratʃni: poplatɛk]
entrance	vchod (m)	[vɦod]
pavilion, hall	pavilón (m)	[pawilo:n]
to register (vt)	registrovat	[rɛgistrovat]
badge (identity tag)	jmenovka (f)	[jmɛnovka]
stand	stánek (m)	[sta:nɛk]
to reserve, to book	rezervovat	[rɛzɛrvovat]
display case	výloha (f)	[vɪːloga]
spotlight	svítidlo (n)	[swi:tidlo]
design	design (m)	[dɪzajn]
to place (put, set)	rozmisťovat	[rozmistɜvat]
distributor	distributor (m)	[dɪstributor]
supplier	dodavatel (m)	[dodavatɛl]
country	země (f)	[zɛmne]
foreign (adj)	zahraniční	[zagranitʃni:]
product	produkt (m)	[produkt]
association	asociace (f)	[asotsijatse]

conference hall	konferenční sál (m)	[konfɛrɛntʃni: sa:l]
congress	kongres (m)	[koŋrɛs]
contest (competition)	soutěž (f)	[soutɛʒ]

visitor	návštěvník (m)	[na:vʃtevni:k]
to visit (attend)	navštěvovat	[navʃtevovat]
customer	zákazník (m)	[za:kazni:k]

84. Science. Research. Scientists

science	věda (f)	[vʰeda]
scientific (adj)	vědecký	[vʰedɛtskɪ:]
scientist	vědec (m)	[vʰedɛts]
theory	teorie (f)	[tɛorije]

axiom	axiom (m)	[aksio:m]
analysis	analýza (f)	[anali:za]
to analyse (vt)	analyzovat	[analizovat]
argument (reasoning)	argument (m)	[argumɛnt]
substance (matter)	látka (f)	[la:tka]

hypothesis	hypotéza (f)	[gipotɛ:za]
dilemma	dilema (n)	[dilɛma]
dissertation	disertace (f)	[dɪsɛrtatse]
dogma	dogma (n)	[dogma]

doctrine	doktrína (f)	[doktri:na]
research	výzkum (m)	[vɪ:skum]
to do research	zkoumat	[skoumat]
testing	kontrola (f)	[kontrola]
laboratory	laboratoř (f)	[laboratorʒ]

method	metoda (f)	[mɛtoda]
molecule	molekula (f)	[molɛkula]
monitoring	monitorování (n)	[monitorova:ni:]
discovery (act, event)	objev (m)	[obʰef]

postulate	postulát (m)	[postula:t]
principle	princip (m)	[prinʦip]
forecast	prognóza (f)	[progno:za]
to forecast (vt)	předpovídat	[prʒedpowi:dat]

synthesis	syntéza (f)	[sintɛ:za]
trend (tendency)	tendence (f)	[tɛndɛnʦe]
theorem	teorém (n)	[tɛorɛ:m]

teachings	nauka (f)	[nauka]
fact	fakt (m)	[fakt]
expedition	výprava (f)	[vɪ:prava]
experiment	experiment (m)	[ɛkspɛrimɛnt]

academician	akademik (m)	[akadɛmik]
bachelor (e.g. ~ of Arts)	bakalář (m)	[bakala:rʃ]
doctor (PhD)	doktor (m)	[doktor]

Associate Professor	docent (m)	[dotsɛnt]
Master (e.g. ~ of Arts)	magistr (m)	[magistr]
professor	profesor (m)	[profɛsor]

Professions and occupations

85. Job search. Dismissal

job	práce (f)	[pra:tse]
personnel	stálí zaměstnanci (m pl)	[sta:li: zamnestnantsi]
career	kariéra (f)	[karije:ra]
prospect	vyhlídky (f pl)	[vɪgli:dkɪ]
skills (expertise)	dovednost (f)	[dovɛdnost]
selection (for job)	výběr (m)	[vɪ:bʰer]
employment agency	kádrová kancelář (f)	[ka:drova: kantsela:rʒ]
curriculum vitae, CV	resumé (n)	[rɛzimɛ:]
interview (for job)	pohovor (m)	[pogovor]
vacancy	neobsazené místo (n)	[nɛobsazɛnɛ: mi:sto]
salary, pay	plat (m), mzda (f)	[plat], [mzda]
fixed salary	stálý plat (m)	[stalɪ plat]
pay, compensation	platba (f)	[platba]
position (job)	funkce (f)	[fuŋktsɛ]
duty (of employee)	povinnost (f)	[powinost]
range of duties	okruh (m)	[okruɦ]
busy (I'm ~)	zaměstnaný	[zamnestnanɪ:]
to fire (dismiss)	propustit	[propustit]
dismissal	propuštění (n)	[propuʃteni:]
unemployment	nezaměstnanost (f)	[nɛzamnestnanost]
unemployed (n)	nezaměstnaný (m)	[nɛzamnestnanɪ:]
retirement	důchod (m)	[du:ɦod]
to retire (from job)	odejít do důchodu	[odɛjɪ:t do du:ɦodu]

86. Business people

director	ředitel (m)	[rʒeditɛl]
manager (director)	správce (m)	[spra:vtse]
boss	šéf (m)	[ʃɛ:f]
superior	vedoucí (m)	[vɛdoutsi:]
superiors	vedení (n)	[vɛdɛni:]
president	prezident (m)	[prɛzidɛnt]
chairman	předseda (m)	[prʃɛdsɛda]
deputy (substitute)	náměstek (m)	[na:mnestɛk]
assistant	pomocník (m)	[pomotsni:k]
secretary	tajemník (m)	[tajemni:k]

personal assistant	osobní tajemník (m)	[osobni: tajemni:k]
businessman	byznysmen (m)	[biznismen]
entrepreneur	podnikatel (m)	[podnikatɛl]
founder	zakladatel (m)	[zakladatɛl]
to found (vt)	založit	[zaloʒit]

founding member	zakladatel (m)	[zakladatɛl]
partner	partner (m)	[partnɛr]
shareholder	akcionář (m)	[aktsijona:rʒ]

millionaire	milionář (m)	[milijona:rʒ]
billionaire	miliardář (m)	[miliarda:rʒ]
owner, proprietor	majitel (m)	[majɪtɛl]
landowner	vlastník (m) půdy	[vlastni:k pu:dɪ]

client	klient (m)	[klijent]
regular client	stálý zákazník (m)	[sta:lɪ: za:kazni:k]
buyer (customer)	zákazník (m)	[za:kazni:k]
visitor	návštěvník (m)	[na:vʃtevni:k]

professional (n)	profesionál (m)	[profɛsijona:l]
expert	znalec (m)	[znalɛts]
specialist	odborník (m)	[odborni:k]

| banker | bankéř (m) | [baŋkɛ:rʒ] |
| broker | broker (m) | [brokɛr] |

cashier	pokladník (m)	[pokladni:k]
accountant	účetní (m, f)	[u:tʃetni:]
security guard	strážce (m)	[stra:ʒtse]

investor	investor (m)	[invɛstor]
debtor	dlužník (m)	[dluʒni:k]
creditor	věřitel (m)	[vʰerʒitɛl]
borrower	vypůjčovatel (m)	[vɪpu:jtʃovatɛl]

| importer | dovozce (m) | [dovoztse] |
| exporter | vývozce (m) | [vɪ:voztse] |

manufacturer	výrobce (m)	[vɪ:robtse]
distributor	distributor (m)	[dɪstributor]
middleman	zprostředkovatel (m)	[sprostrʃɛdkovatɛl]

consultant	konzultant (m)	[konzultant]
representative	zástupce (m)	[za:stuptse]
agent	agent (m)	[agɛnt]
insurance agent	pojišťovací agent (m)	[pojɪʃtɜvatsi: agɛnt]

87. Service professions

cook	kuchař (m)	[kuɦarʒ]
chef	šéfkuchař (m)	[ʃɛ:fkuɦarʒ]
baker	pekař (m)	[pɛkarʒ]
barman	barman (m)	[barman]

| waiter | číšník (m) | [ʧiːʃniːk] |
| waitress | číšnice (f) | [ʧiːʃnitse] |

lawyer, barrister	advokát (m)	[advokaːt]
lawyer (legal expert)	právník (m)	[praːvniːk]
notary	notář (m)	[notaːrʒ]

electrician	elektromontér (m)	[ɛlɛktromontɛːr]
plumber	instalatér (m)	[instalatɛːr]
carpenter	tesař (m)	[tɛsarʒ]

masseur	masér (m)	[masɛːr]
masseuse	masérka (f)	[masɛːrka]
doctor	lékař (m)	[lɛːkarʒ]

taxi driver	taxikář (m)	[taksikaːrʒ]
driver	řidič (m)	[rʒidiʧ]
delivery man	kurýr (m)	[kuriːr]

chambermaid	pokojská (f)	[pokojskaː]
security guard	strážce (m)	[straːʒtse]
stewardess	letuška (f)	[lɛtuʃka]

teacher (in primary school)	učitel (m)	[uʧitɛl]
librarian	knihovník (m)	[knigovniːk]
translator	překladatel (m)	[prʃɛkladatɛl]
interpreter	tlumočník (m)	[tlumoʧniːk]
guide	průvodce (m)	[pruːvodtse]

hairdresser	holič (m) / kadeřník (m)	[goliʧ] / [kadɛrʒniːk]
postman	listonoš (m)	[listonoʃ]
shop assistant (masc.)	prodavač (m)	[prodavaʧ]

gardener	zahradník (m)	[zagradniːk]
servant (in household)	sluha (m)	[sluga]
maid	služka (f)	[sluʒka]
cleaner (cleaning lady)	uklízečka (f)	[ukliːzɛʧka]

88. Military professions and ranks

private	vojín (m)	[vojiːn]
sergeant	seržant (m)	[sɛrʒant]
lieutenant	poručík (m)	[poruʧiːk]
captain	kapitán (m)	[kapitaːn]

major	major (m)	[major]
colonel	plukovník (m)	[plukovniːk]
general	generál (m)	[gɛnɛraːl]
marshal	maršál (m)	[marʃaːl]
admiral	admirál (m)	[admiraːl]

military man	voják (m)	[vojaːk]
soldier	voják (m)	[vojaːk]
officer	důstojník (m)	[duːstojniːk]

commander	velitel (m)	[vɛlitɛl]
border guard	pohraničník (m)	[pograniʧniːk]
radio operator	radista (m)	[radista]
scout (searcher)	rozvědčík (m)	[rozvʰedʧiːk]
pioneer (sapper)	ženista (m)	[ʒenɪsta]
marksman	střelec (m)	[strʃɛlɛʦ]
navigator	navigátor (m)	[nawiga:tor]

89. Officials. Priests

king	král (m)	[kraːl]
queen	královna (f)	[kraːlovna]

prince	princ (m)	[prinʦ]
princess	princezna (f)	[prinʦezna]

tsar, czar	car (m)	[ʦar]
czarina	carevna (f)	[ʦarɛvna]

president	prezident (m)	[prɛzidɛnt]
Minister	ministr (m)	[minɪstr]
prime minister	premiér (m)	[prɛmijeːr]
senator	senátor (m)	[sɛnaːtor]

diplomat	diplomat (m)	[dɪplomat]
consul	konzul (m)	[konzul]
ambassador	velvyslanec (m)	[vɛlvɪslanɛʦ]
advisor (military ~)	rada (m)	[rada]

official (civil servant)	úředník (m)	[uːrʒedniːk]
prefect	prefekt (m)	[prɛfɛkt]
mayor	primátor (m)	[primaːtor]

judge	soudce (m)	[soudʦe]
prosecutor	prokurátor (m)	[prokuraːtor]

missionary	misionář (m)	[misijonaːrʒ]
monk	mnich (m)	[mniɦ]
abbot	opat (m)	[opat]
rabbi	rabín (m)	[rabiːn]

vizier	vezír (m)	[vɛziːr]
shah	šach (m)	[ʃaɦ]
sheikh	šejk (m)	[ʃɛjk]

90. Agricultural professions

beekeeper	včelař (m)	[vʧelarʒ]
herdsman	pasák (m)	[pasaːk]
agronomist	agronom (m)	[agronom]
cattle breeder	chovatel (m)	[ɦovatɛl]
veterinary surgeon	zvěrolékař (m)	[zvʰerolɛːkarʒ]

farmer	farmář (m)	[farma:rʒ]
winemaker	vinař (m)	[winarʒ]
zoologist	zoolog (m)	[zo:log]
cowboy	kovboj (m)	[kovboj]

91. Art professions

actor	herec (m)	[gɛrɛʦ]
actress	herečka (f)	[gɛrɛʧka]

singer (masc.)	zpěvák (m)	[spʰeva:k]
singer (fem.)	zpěvačka (f)	[spʰevaʧka]

dancer (masc.)	tanečník (m)	[tanɛʧni:k]
dancer (fem.)	tanečnice (f)	[tanɛʧnitse]

performing artist (masc.)	herec (m)	[gɛrɛʦ]
performing artist (fem.)	herečka (f)	[gɛrɛʧka]

musician	hudebník (m)	[gudɛbni:k]
pianist	klavírista (m)	[klawi:rista]
guitar player	kytarista (m)	[kɪtarista]

conductor (of musicians)	dirigent (m)	[dɪrigɛnt]
composer	skladatel (m)	[skladatɛl]
impresario	impresário (m)	[imprɛsa:rio]

film director	režisér (m)	[rɛʒisɛ:r]
producer	filmový producent (m)	[filmovɪ: produʦent]
scriptwriter	scenárista (m)	[sʦena:rista]
critic	kritik (m)	[kritɪk]

writer	spisovatel (m)	[spisovatɛl]
poet	básník (m)	[ba:sni:k]
sculptor	sochař (m)	[soɦarʒ]
artist (painter)	malíř (m)	[mali:rʒ]

juggler	žonglér (m)	[ʒoŋlɛ:r]
clown	klaun (m)	[klaun]
acrobat	akrobat (m)	[akrobat]
magician	kouzelník (m)	[kouzɛlni:k]

92. Various professions

doctor	lékař (m)	[lɛ:karʒ]
nurse	zdravotní sestra (f)	[zdravotni: sɛstra]
psychiatrist	psychiatr (m)	[psiɦijatr]
stomatologist	stomatolog (m)	[stomatolog]
surgeon	chirurg (m)	[ɦirurg]

astronaut	astronaut (m)	[astronaut]
astronomer	astronom (m)	[astronom]

driver (of taxi, etc.)	řidič (m)	[rʒidiʧ]
train driver	strojvůdce (m)	[strojvu:dtse]
mechanic	mechanik (m)	[mɛɦanɪk]

miner	horník (m)	[gorni:k]
worker	dělník (m)	[delni:k]
metalworker	zámečník (m)	[za:mɛʧni:k]
carpenter	truhlář (m)	[trugla:rʒ]
turner	soustružník (m)	[soustruʒni:k]
building worker	stavitel (m)	[stawitɛl]
welder	svářeč (m)	[sva:rʒeʧ]

professor (title)	profesor (m)	[profɛsor]
architect	architekt (m)	[arɦitɛkt]
historian	historik (m)	[gistorik]
scientist	vědec (m)	[vʰedɛʦ]
physicist	fyzik (m)	[fizik]
chemist (scientist)	chemik (m)	[ɦɛmik]

archaeologist	archeolog (m)	[arɦɛolog]
geologist	geolog (m)	[gɛolog]
researcher	výzkumník (m)	[vɪ:skumni:k]

| babysitter | chůva (f) | [ɦu:va] |
| teacher, educator | pedagog (m) | [pɛdagog] |

editor	redaktor (m)	[rɛdaktor]
editor-in-chief	šéfredaktor (m)	[ʃɛ:frɛdaktor]
correspondent	zpravodaj (m)	[spravodaj]
typist (fem.)	písařka (f)	[pi:sarʒka]

designer	návrhář (m)	[na:vrga:rʒ]
computer expert	odborník (m) na počítače	[odborni:k na potʃi:tatʃe]
programmer	programátor (m)	[programa:tor]
engineer (designer)	inženýr (m)	[inʒenɪ:r]

sailor	námořník (m)	[na:morʒni:k]
seaman	námořník (m)	[na:morʒni:k]
rescuer	záchranář (m)	[za:ɦrana:rʒ]

firefighter	hasič (m)	[gasiʧ]
policeman	policista (m)	[poliʦista]
watchman	hlídač (m)	[gli:daʧ]
detective	detektiv (m)	[dɛtɛktɪv]

customs officer	celník (m)	[ʦelni:k]
bodyguard	osobní strážce (m)	[osobni: stra:ʒtse]
prison officer	dozorce (m)	[dozortse]
inspector	inspektor (m)	[inspɛktor]

sportsman	sportovec (m)	[sportovɛʦ]
trainer, coach	trenér (m)	[trɛnɛ:r]
butcher	řezník (m)	[rʒezni:k]
cobbler	obuvník (m)	[obuvni:k]
merchant	obchodník (m)	[obɦodni:k]
loader (person)	nakládač (m)	[nakla:daʧ]

| fashion designer | modelář (m) | [modɛla:rʒ] |
| model (fem.) | modelka (f) | [modɛlka] |

93. Occupations. Social status

| schoolboy | žák (m) | [ʒa:k] |
| student (college ~) | student (m) | [studɛnt] |

philosopher	filozof (m)	[filozof]
economist	ekonom (m)	[ɛkonom]
inventor	vynálezce (m)	[vɪna:lɛzʦe]

unemployed (n)	nezaměstnaný (m)	[nɛzamnestnanɪ:]
pensioner	důchodce (m)	[du:ɦodʦe]
spy, secret agent	špión (m)	[ʃpijo:n]

prisoner	vězeň (m)	[vʰezɛɲ]
striker	stávkující (m)	[sta:vkujɪ:ʦi:]
bureaucrat	byrokrat (m)	[birokrat]
traveller	cestovatel (m)	[ʦestovatɛl]

| homosexual | homosexuál (m) | [gomosɛksua:l] |
| hacker | hacker (m) | [gɛkr] |

bandit	bandita (m)	[bandɪta]
hit man, killer	najatý vrah (m)	[najatɪ: vraɦ]
drug addict	narkoman (m)	[narkoman]
drug dealer	drogový dealer (m)	[drogovɪ: dɪ:lɛr]
prostitute (fem.)	prostitutka (f)	[prostɪtutka]
pimp	kuplíř (m)	[kupli:rʒ]

sorcerer	čaroděj (m)	[ʧarodej]
sorceress	čarodějka (f)	[ʧarodejka]
pirate	pirát (m)	[pira:t]
slave	otrok (m)	[otrok]
samurai	samuraj (m)	[samuraj]
savage (primitive)	divoch (m)	[divoɦ]

Education

94. School

school	škola (f)	[ʃkola]
headmaster	ředitel (m) školy	[rʒeditɛl ʃkolɪ]
pupil (boy)	žák (m)	[ʒaːk]
pupil (girl)	žákyně (f)	[ʒaːkɪne]
schoolboy	žák (m)	[ʒaːk]
schoolgirl	žákyně (f)	[ʒaːkɪne]
to teach (sb)	učit	[utʃit]
to learn (language, etc.)	učit se	[utʃit sɛ]
to learn by heart	učit se nazpaměť	[utʃit sɛ naspamnetⁱ]
to study (work to learn)	učit se	[utʃit sɛ]
to be at school	učit se	[utʃit sɛ]
to go to school	jít do školy	[jɪːt do ʃkolɪ]
alphabet	abeceda (f)	[abɛtseda]
subject (at school)	předmět (m)	[prʃɛdmnet]
classroom	třída (f)	[trʃiːda]
lesson	hodina (f)	[godina]
playtime, break	přestávka (f)	[prʃɛstaːvka]
school bell	zvonění (n)	[zvoneni:]
desk (for pupil)	školní lavice (f)	[ʃkolni: lawitse]
blackboard	tabule (f)	[tabulɛ]
mark	známka (f)	[znaːmka]
good mark	dobrá známka (f)	[dobra: znaːmka]
bad mark	špatná známka (f)	[ʃpatna: znaːmka]
to give a mark	dávat známku	[daːvat znaːmku]
mistake	chyba (f)	[ɦɪba]
to make mistakes	dělat chyby	[delat ɦɪbɪ]
to correct (an error)	opravovat	[opravovat]
crib	tahák (m)	[tagaːk]
homework	domácí úloha (f)	[domaːtsi: uːloga]
exercise (in education)	cvičení (n)	[tswitʃeni:]
to be present	být přítomen	[bɪːt prʃiːtomɛn]
to be absent	chybět	[ɦɪbʰet]
to punish (vt)	trestat	[trɛstat]
punishment	trest (m)	[trɛst]
conduct (behaviour)	chování (n)	[ɦovaːni:]

school report	žákovská knížka (f)	[ʒaːkovska: kniːʒka]
pencil	tužka (f)	[tuʃka]
rubber	guma (f)	[guma]
chalk	křída (f)	[krʃiːda]
pencil case	penál (m)	[pɛnaːl]

schoolbag	brašna (f)	[braʃna]
pen	pero (n)	[pɛro]
exercise book	sešit (m)	[sɛʃit]
textbook	učebnice (f)	[utʃebnitse]
compasses	kružidlo (n)	[kruʒidlo]

| to draw (a blueprint, etc.) | rýsovat | [riːsovat] |
| technical drawing | výkres (m) | [viːkrɛs] |

poem	báseň (f)	[baːsɛɲ]
by heart (adv)	nazpaměť	[naspamnetⁱ]
to learn by heart	učit se nazpaměť	[utʃit sɛ naspamnetⁱ]

| school holidays | prázdniny (f pl) | [praːzdninɪ] |
| to be on holiday | mít prázdniny | [miːt praːzdninɪ] |

test (at school)	písemka (f)	[piːsɛmka]
essay (composition)	sloh (m)	[sloɦ]
dictation	diktát (m)	[dɪktaːt]

exam	zkouška (f)	[skouʃka]
to take an exam	dělat zkoušky	[delat skouʃkɪ]
experiment (chemical ~)	pokus (m)	[pokus]

95. College. University

academy	akademie (f)	[akadɛmije]
university	univerzita (f)	[unɪvɛrzita]
faculty (section)	fakulta (f)	[fakulta]

student (masc.)	student (m)	[studɛnt]
student (fem.)	studentka (f)	[studɛntka]
lecturer (teacher)	vyučující (m)	[vɪutʃujɪːtsi:]

| lecture hall, room | posluchárna (f) | [posluɦaːrna] |
| graduate | absolvent (m) | [absolvɛnt] |

| diploma | diplom (m) | [dɪplom] |
| dissertation | disertace (f) | [dɪsɛrtatse] |

| study (report) | bádání (n) | [baːdaːni:] |
| laboratory | laboratoř (f) | [laboratorʒ] |

| lecture | přednáška (f) | [prʃɛdnaːʃka] |
| course mate | spolužák (m) | [spoluʒaːk] |

| scholarship | stipendium (n) | [stɪpɛndɪjum] |
| academic degree | akademická hodnost (f) | [akadɛmitska: godnost] |

96. Sciences. Disciplines

mathematics	matematika (f)	[matɛmatika]
algebra	algebra (f)	[algɛbra]
geometry	geometrie (f)	[gɛomɛtrije]
astronomy	astronomie (f)	[astronomije]
biology	biologie (f)	[bijologije]
geography	zeměpis (m)	[zɛmnepis]
geology	geologie (f)	[gɛologije]
history	historie (f)	[gistorije]
medicine	lékařství (n)	[lɛ:karʃstwi:]
pedagogy	pedagogika (f)	[pɛdagogika]
law	právo (n)	[pra:vo]
physics	fyzika (f)	[fizika]
chemistry	chemie (f)	[ɦɛmije]
philosophy	filozofie (f)	[filozofije]
psychology	psychologie (f)	[psiɦologije]

97. Writing system. Orthography

grammar	mluvnice (f)	[mluvnitsɛ]
vocabulary	slovní zásoba (f)	[slovni: za:soba]
phonetics	hláskosloví (n)	[gla:skoslowi:]
noun	podstatné jméno (n)	[podsta:tnɛ: jmɛ:no]
adjective	přídavné jméno (n)	[prʃi:davnɛ: jmɛ:no]
verb	sloveso (n)	[slovɛso]
adverb	příslovce (n)	[prʃi:slovtsɛ]
pronoun	zájmeno (n)	[za:jmɛno]
interjection	citoslovce (n)	[tsitoslovtsɛ]
preposition	předložka (f)	[prʃɛdloʒka]
root	slovní základ (m)	[slovni: za:klad]
ending	koncovka (f)	[kontsovka]
prefix	předpona (f)	[prʃɛdpona]
syllable	slabika (f)	[slabika]
suffix	přípona (f)	[prʃi:pona]
stress mark	přízvuk (m)	[prʃi:zvuk]
apostrophe	odsuvník (m)	[odsuvni:k]
full stop	tečka (f)	[tɛtʃka]
comma	čárka (f)	[tʃa:rka]
semicolon	středník (m)	[strʃɛdni:k]
colon	dvojtečka (f)	[dvojtɛtʃka]
ellipsis	tři tečky (f pl)	[trʃi tɛtʃkɪ]
question mark	otazník (m)	[otazni:k]
exclamation mark	vykřičník (m)	[vɪkrʃitʃni:k]

inverted commas	uvozovky (f pl)	[uvozovkɪ]
in inverted commas	v uvozovkách	[f uvozovka:ɦ]
parenthesis	závorky (f pl)	[za:vorkɪ]
in parenthesis	v závorkách	[v za:vorkaɦ]

hyphen	spojovník (m)	[spojovni:k]
dash	pomlčka (f)	[pomlʧka]
space (between words)	mezera (f)	[mɛzɛra]

| letter | písmeno (n) | [pi:smɛno] |
| capital letter | velké písmeno (n) | [vɛlkɛ: pi:smɛno] |

| vowel (n) | samohláska (f) | [samogla:ska] |
| consonant (n) | souhláska (f) | [sougla:ska] |

sentence	věta (f)	[vʰeta]
subject	podmět (m)	[podmnet]
predicate	přísudek (m)	[prʃi:sudɛk]

line	řádek (m)	[rʒa:dɛk]
on a new line	z nového řádku	[z novɛ:go rʒa:dku]
paragraph	odstavec (m)	[odstavɛʦ]

word	slovo (n)	[slovo]
word group	slovní spojení (n)	[slovni: spojeni:]
expression	výraz (m)	[vɪ:raz]
synonym	synonymum (n)	[sinonɪmum]
antonym	antonymum (n)	[antonɪmum]

rule	pravidlo (n)	[prawidlo]
exception	výjimka (f)	[vɪ:jɪmka]
correct (adj)	správný	[spra:vnɪ:]

conjugation	časování (n)	[ʧasova:ni:]
declension	skloňování (n)	[sklonʒva:ni:]
nominal case	pád (m)	[pa:d]
question	otázka (f)	[ota:zka]
to underline (vt)	podtrhnout	[podtrgnout]
dotted line	tečkování (n)	[tɛʧkova:ni:]

98. Foreign languages

language	jazyk (m)	[jazɪk]
foreign language	cizí jazyk (m)	[ʦizi: jazɪk]
to study (vt)	studovat	[studovat]
to learn (language, etc.)	učit se	[uʧit sɛ]

to read (vi, vt)	číst	[ʧi:st]
to speak (vi, vt)	mluvit	[mluwit]
to understand (vt)	rozumět	[rozumnet]
to write (vt)	psát	[psa:t]

| fast (adv) | rychle | [rɪɦlɛ] |
| slowly (adv) | pomalu | [pomalu] |

fluently (adv)	plynně	[plɪŋe]
rules	pravidla (n pl)	[prawidla]
grammar	mluvnice (f)	[mluvnitse]
vocabulary	slovní zásoba (f)	[slovni: za:soba]
phonetics	hláskosloví (n)	[gla:skoslowi:]

textbook	učebnice (f)	[utʃebnitse]
dictionary	slovník (m)	[slovni:k]
teach-yourself book	učebnice (f) pro samouky	[utʃebnitse pro samoukɪ]
phrasebook	konverzace (f)	[konvɛrzatse]

cassette	kazeta (f)	[kazɛta]
videotape	videokazeta (f)	[widɛokazɛta]
CD, compact disc	CD disk (m)	[tsedɛ dɪsk]
DVD	DVD (n)	[dɛvɛdɛ]

alphabet	abeceda (f)	[abɛtseda]
to spell (vt)	hláskovat	[gla:skovat]
pronunciation	výslovnost (f)	[vɪ:slovnost]

accent	cizí přízvuk (m)	[tsizi: prʃi:zvuk]
with an accent	s cizím přízvukem	[s tsizi:m prʃi:zvukɛm]
without an accent	bez cizího přízvuku	[bɛz tsizi:go prʃi:zvuku]

| word | slovo (n) | [slovo] |
| meaning | smysl (m) | [smɪsl] |

course (e.g. a French ~)	kurzy (m pl)	[kurzɪ]
to sign up	zapsat se	[zapsat sɛ]
teacher	vyučující (m)	[vɪutʃujɪ:tsi:]

translation (process)	překlad (m)	[prʃɛklad]
translation (text, etc.)	překlad (m)	[prʃɛklad]
translator	překladatel (m)	[prʃɛkladatɛl]
interpreter	tlumočník (m)	[tlumotʃni:k]

| polyglot | polyglot (m) | [poliglot] |
| memory | paměť (f) | [pamnetʲ] |

Rest. Entertainment. Travel

99. Trip. Travel

tourism	turistika (f)	[turɪstɪka]
tourist	turista (m)	[turista]
trip, voyage	cestování (n)	[tsestovaːniː]
adventure	příhoda (f)	[prʃiːgoda]
trip, journey	cesta (f)	[tsesta]
holiday	dovolená (f)	[dovolɛnaː]
to be on holiday	mít dovolenou	[miːt dovolɛːnou]
rest	odpočinek (m)	[odpotʃinɛk]
train	vlak (m)	[vlak]
by train	vlakem	[vlakɛm]
aeroplane	letadlo (n)	[lɛtadlo]
by aeroplane	letadlem	[lɛtadlɛm]
by car	autem	[autɛm]
by ship	lodí	[lodiː]
luggage	zavazadla (n pl)	[zavazadla]
suitcase, luggage	kufr (m)	[kufr]
luggage trolley	vozík (m) na zavazadla	[voziːk na zavazadla]
passport	pas (m)	[pas]
visa	vízum (n)	[wiːzum]
ticket	jízdenka (f)	[jɪːzdɛŋka]
air ticket	letenka (f)	[lɛtɛŋka]
guidebook	průvodce (m)	[pruːvodtsɛ]
map	mapa (f)	[mapa]
area (rural ~)	krajina (f)	[krajɪna]
place, site	místo (n)	[miːsto]
exotica	exotika (f)	[ɛgzotɪka]
exotic (adj)	exotický	[ɛgzotɪtskɪː]
amazing (adj)	podivuhodný	[podivugodnɪː]
group	skupina (f)	[skupina]
excursion	výlet (m)	[vɪːlɛt]
guide (person)	průvodce (m)	[pruːvodtsɛ]

100. Hotel

hotel	hotel (m)	[gotɛl]
motel	motel (m)	[motɛl]
three-star (adj)	tři hvězdy	[trʃi gvʰezdɪ]

| five-star | pět hvězd | [pʰet gvʰezd] |
| to stay (in hotel, etc.) | ubytovat se | [ubɪtovat sɛ] |

room	pokoj (m)	[pokoj]
single room	jednolůžkový pokoj (m)	[jednolu:ʒkovɪ: pokoj]
double room	dvoulůžkový pokoj (m)	[dvoulu:ʒkovɪ: pokoj]
to book a room	rezervovat pokoj	[rɛzɛrvovat pokoj]

| half board | polopenze (f) | [polopɛnzɛ] |
| full board | plná penze (f) | [plna: pɛnzɛ] |

with bath	s koupelnou	[s koupɛlnou]
with shower	se sprchou	[sɛ sprɦou]
satellite television	satelitní televize (f)	[satɛlitni: tɛlɛwizɛ]
air-conditioner	klimatizátor (m)	[klimatiza:tor]
towel	ručník (m)	[rutʃni:k]
key	klíč (m)	[kli:tʃ]

administrator	recepční (m)	[rɛtseptʃni:]
chambermaid	pokojská (f)	[pokojska:]
porter, bellboy	nosič (m)	[nositʃ]
doorman	vrátný (m)	[vra:tnɪ:]

restaurant	restaurace (f)	[rɛstauratse]
pub, bar	bar (m)	[bar]
breakfast	snídaně (f)	[sni:dane]
dinner	večeře (f)	[vɛtʃerʒe]
buffet	obložený stůl (m)	[oblɔʒenɪ: stu:l]

| lobby | vstupní hala (f) | [vstupni: gala] |
| lift | výtah (m) | [vɪ:taɦ] |

| DO NOT DISTURB | NERUŠIT | [nɛruʃit] |
| NO SMOKING | ZÁKAZ KOUŘENÍ | [za:kaz kourʒeni:] |

Technical equipment

101. Computer

computer	počítač (m)	[potʃi:tatʃ]
notebook, laptop	notebook (m)	[noutbu:k]
to switch on	zapnout	[zapnout]
to turn off	vypnout	[vɪpnout]
keyboard	klávesnice (f)	[kla:vɛsnitse]
key	klávesa (f)	[kla:vɛsa]
mouse	myš (f)	[mɪʃ]
mouse mat	podložka (f) pro myš	[podloʒka pro mɪʃ]
button	tlačítko (n)	[tlatʃi:tko]
cursor	kurzor (m)	[kurzor]
monitor	monitor (m)	[monɪtor]
screen	obrazovka (f)	[obrazovka]
hard disk	pevný disk (m)	[pɛvnɪ: dɪsk]
hard disk volume	rozměr (m) disku	[rozmner dɪsku]
memory	paměť (f)	[pamnetʲ]
random access memory	operační paměť (f)	[opɛratʃni: pamnetʲ]
file	soubor (m)	[soubor]
folder	složka (f)	[sloʒka]
to open (vt)	otevřít	[otɛvrʒi:t]
to close (vt)	zavřít	[zavrʒi:t]
to save (vt)	uložit	[uloʒit]
to delete (vt)	vymazat	[vɪmazat]
to copy (vt)	zkopírovat	[skopi:rovat]
to sort (vt)	uspořádat	[usporʒa:dat]
to transfer (copy)	zkopírovat	[skopi:rovat]
programme	program (m)	[program]
software	programové vybavení (n)	[programovɛ: vɪbavɛni:]
programmer	programátor (m)	[programa:tor]
to program (vt)	programovat	[programovat]
hacker	hacker (m)	[gɛkr]
password	heslo (n)	[gɛslo]
virus	virus (m)	[wirus]
to find, to detect	zjistit	[zʰjɪstit]
byte	byte (m)	[bajt]
megabyte	megabyte (m)	[mɛgabajt]
data	data (n pl)	[data]

| database | databáze (f) | [databa:zɛ] |
| cable (wire) | kabel (m) | [kabɛl] |

| to disconnect (vt) | odpojit | [odpojɪt] |
| to connect (sth to sth) | připojit | [prʃɪpojɪt] |

102. Internet. E-mail

| Internet | internet (m) | [intɛrnɛt] |
| browser | prohlížeč (m) | [progli:ʒeʧ] |

| search engine | vyhledávací zdroj (m) | [vɪglɛda:vaʦi: zdroj] |
| provider | dodavatel (m) | [dodavatɛl] |

web master	web-master (m)	[vɛbmastɛr]
website	webové stránky (f pl)	[vɛbove: stra:ŋkɪ]
web page	webová stránka (f)	[vɛbova: stra:ŋka]

| address | adresa (f) | [adrɛsa] |
| address book | adresář (m) | [adrɛsa:rʒ] |

| postbox | poštovní schránka (f) | [poʃtovni: sɦra:ŋka] |
| post | pošta (f) | [poʃta] |

message	zpráva (f)	[spra:va]
sender	odesílatel (m)	[odɛsi:latɛl]
to send (vt)	odeslat	[odɛslat]
sending (of mail)	odeslání (n)	[odɛsla:ni:]

| receiver | příjemce (m) | [prʃi:jemʦe] |
| to receive (vt) | dostat | [dostat] |

| correspondence | korespondence (f) | [korɛspondɛnʦe] |
| to correspond (vi) | korespondovat | [korɛspondovat] |

file	soubor (m)	[soubor]
to download (vt)	stáhnout	[sta:gnout]
to create (vt)	vytvořit	[vɪtvorʒit]

| to delete (vt) | vymazat | [vɪmazat] |
| deleted (adj) | vymazaný | [vɪmazanɪ:] |

connection (ADSL, etc.)	spojení (n)	[spojeni:]
speed	rychlost (f)	[rɪɦlost]
modem	modem (m)	[modɛm]

| access | přístup (m) | [prʃi:stup] |
| port (e.g. input ~) | port (m) | [port] |

| connection (make a ~) | připojení (n) | [prʃipojeni:] |
| to connect (vi) | připojit se | [prʃipojɪt sɛ] |

| to select (vt) | vybrat | [vɪbrat] |
| to search (for ...) | hledat | [glɛdat] |

103. Electricity

electricity	elektřina (f)	[ɛlɛktrʃina]
electrical (adj)	elektrický	[ɛlɛktritskɪ:]
electric power station	elektrárna (f)	[ɛlɛktra:rna]
energy	energie (f)	[ɛnɛrgije]
electric power	elektrická energie (f)	[ɛlɛktritska: ɛnɛrgije]
light bulb	žárovka (f)	[ʒa:rovka]
torch	baterka (f)	[batɛrka]
street light	pouliční lampa (f)	[poulitʃni: lampa]
light	světlo (n)	[svʰetlo]
to turn on	zapínat	[zapi:nat]
to turn off	vypínat	[vɪpi:nat]
to turn off the light	zhasnout světlo	[zgasnout svʰetlo]
to burn out (vi)	přepálit se	[prʃɛpa:lit sɛ]
short circuit	krátké spojení (n)	[kra:tkɛ: spojeni:]
broken wire	přetržení (n)	[prʃɛtrʒeni:]
contact	kontakt (m)	[kontakt]
light switch	vypínač (m)	[vɪpi:natʃ]
socket outlet	zásuvka (f)	[za:suvka]
plug	zástrčka (f)	[za:strtʃka]
extension lead	prodlužovák (m)	[prodluʒova:k]
fuse	pojistka (f)	[pojɪstka]
cable, wire	vodič (m)	[voditʃ]
wiring	vedení (n)	[vɛdɛni:]
ampere	ampér (m)	[ampɛ:r]
amperage	intenzita (f) proudu	[intɛnzita proudu]
volt	volt (m)	[volt]
voltage	napětí (n)	[napʰeti:]
electrical device	elektrický přístroj (m)	[ɛlɛktritskɪ: prʃi:stroj]
indicator	indikátor (m)	[indika:tor]
electrician	elektrotechnik (m)	[ɛlɛktrotɛhnik]
to solder (vt)	letovat	[lɛtovat]
soldering iron	letovačka (f)	[lɛtovatʃka]
electric current	proud (m)	[prout]

104. Tools

tool, instrument	nářadí (n)	[na:rʒadi:]
tools	nástroje (m pl)	[nastroje]
equipment (factory ~)	zařízení (n)	[zarʒi:zɛni:]
hammer	kladivo (n)	[kladivo]
screwdriver	šroubovák (m)	[ʃroubova:k]
axe	sekera (f)	[sɛkɛra]

saw	pila (f)	[pila]
to saw (vt)	řezat	[rʒezat]
plane (tool)	hoblík (m)	[gobliːk]
to plane (vt)	hoblovat	[goblovat]
soldering iron	letovačka (f)	[lɛtovatʃka]
to solder (vt)	letovat	[lɛtovat]

file (for metal)	pilník (m)	[pilniːk]
carpenter pincers	kleště (f pl)	[klɛʃte]
combination pliers	ploché kleště (f pl)	[plohɛː klɛʃte]
chisel	dláto (n)	[dlaːto]

drill bit	vrták (m)	[vrtaːk]
electric drill	svidřík (m)	[swidrʒiːk]
to drill (vi, vt)	vrtat	[vrtat]

knife	nůž (m)	[nuːʒ]
pocket knife	kapesní nůž (m)	[kapɛsniː nuːʒ]
folding (knife, etc.)	skládací	[sklaːdatsiː]
blade	čepel (f)	[tʃepɛl]

sharp (blade, etc.)	ostrý	[ostrɪː]
blunt (adj)	tupý	[tupɪː]
to become blunt	ztupit se	[stupit sɛ]
to sharpen (vt)	ostřit	[ostrʃit]

bolt	šroub (m)	[ʃroub]
nut	matice (f)	[matitse]
thread (of a screw)	závit (m)	[zaːwit]
wood screw	vrut (m)	[vrut]

| nail | hřebík (m) | [grʒebiːk] |
| nailhead | hlavička (f) | [glawitʃka] |

ruler (for measuring)	pravítko (n)	[prawiːtko]
tape measure	měřicí pásmo (n)	[mnerʒitsiː paːsmo]
spirit level	libela (f)	[libɛla]
magnifying glass	lupa (f)	[lupa]

measuring instrument	měřicí přístroj (m)	[mnerʒitsiː prʃiːstroj]
to measure (vt)	měřit	[mnerʒit]
scale (of thermometer, etc.)	stupnice (f)	[stupnitse]
readings	údaje (m pl)	[uːdaje]

| compressor | kompresor (m) | [komprɛsor] |
| microscope | mikroskop (m) | [mikroskop] |

pump (e.g. water ~)	pumpa (f)	[pumpa]
robot	robot (m)	[robot]
laser	laser (m)	[lɛjzr]

spanner	maticový klíč (m)	[matitsovɪ kliːtʃ]
adhesive tape	lepicí páska (f)	[lɛpitsi paːska]
glue	lepidlo (n)	[lɛpidlo]
emery paper	smirkový papír (m)	[smirkovɪ papiːr]
spring	pružina (f)	[pruʒina]

| magnet | magnet (m) | [magnɛt] |
| gloves | rukavice (f pl) | [rukawitse] |

rope	provaz (m)	[provaz]
cord	šňůra (f)	[ʃny:ra]
wire (e.g. telephone ~)	vodič (m)	[voditʃ]
cable	kabel (m)	[kabɛl]

sledgehammer	palice (f)	[palitse]
crowbar	sochor (m)	[soɦor]
ladder	žebřík (m)	[ʒebrʒi:k]
stepladder	dvojitý žebřík (m)	[dvojıtı: ʒebrʒi:k]

to screw (tighten)	zakroutit	[zakroutit]
to unscrew (vt)	odšroubovávat	[odʃroubova:vat]
to tighten (vt)	svírat	[swi:rat]
to glue, to stick	přilepit	[prʃilɛpit]
to cut (vt)	řezat	[rʒezat]

malfunction (fault)	porucha (f)	[poruɦa]
repair (mending)	oprava (f)	[oprava]
to repair, to mend (vt)	opravovat	[opravovat]
to adjust (machine, etc.)	seřizovat	[sɛrʒizovat]

to check (to examine)	zkoušet	[skouʃɛt]
checking	kontrola (f)	[kontrola]
readings	údaj (m)	[u:daj]

| reliable (machine) | spolehlivý | [spolɛglivı:] |
| complicated (adj) | složitý | [sloʒitı:] |

to rust (vi)	rezavět	[rɛzavʰet]
rusty (adj)	rezavý	[rɛzavı:]
rust	rez (f)	[rɛz]

TECHNICAL EQUIPMENT. TRANSPORT

Transport

105. Aeroplane

aeroplane	letadlo (n)	[lɛtadlo]
air ticket	letenka (f)	[lɛtɛŋka]
airline	letecká společnost (f)	[lɛtɛtska: spolɛtʃnost]
airport	letiště (n)	[lɛtiʃte]
supersonic (adj)	nadzvukový	[nadzvukovı:]
captain	velitel (m) posádky	[vɛlitɛl posa:dkı]
crew	posádka (f)	[posa:dka]
pilot	pilot (m)	[pilot]
stewardess	letuška (f)	[lɛtuʃka]
navigator	navigátor (m)	[nawiga:tor]
wings	křídla (n pl)	[krʃi:dla]
tail	ocas (m)	[otsas]
cockpit	kabina (f)	[kabina]
engine	motor (m)	[motor]
undercarriage	podvozek (m)	[podvozɛk]
turbine	turbína (f)	[turbi:na]
propeller	vrtule (f)	[vrtulɛ]
black box	černá skříňka (f)	[tʃerna: skrʃi:ɲka]
control column	řídicí páka (f)	[rʒi:ditsi: pa:ka]
fuel	palivo (n)	[palivo]
safety card	předpis (m)	[prʃɛdpis]
oxygen mask	kyslíková maska (f)	[kısli:kova: maska]
uniform	uniforma (f)	[unıforma]
lifejacket	záchranná vesta (f)	[za:ɦrana: vɛsta]
parachute	padák (m)	[pada:k]
takeoff	start (m) letadla	[start lɛtadla]
to take off (vi)	vzlétat	[vzlɛ:tat]
runway	rozjezdová dráha (f)	[rozʰezdova dra:ga]
visibility	viditelnost (f)	[widitɛlnost]
flight (act of flying)	let (m)	[lɛt]
altitude	výška (f)	[vı:ʃka]
air pocket	vzdušná jáma (f)	[vzduʃna: jama]
seat	místo (n)	[mi:sto]
headphones	sluchátka (n pl)	[sluɦa:tka]
folding tray	odklápěcí stolek (m)	[odkla:pʰetsi: stolɛk]
airplane window	okénko (n)	[okɛ:ŋko]
aisle	chodba (f)	[ɦodba]

98

106. Train

train	vlak (m)	[vlak]
suburban train	vlak (m) elektrické dráhy	[vlak ɛlɛktritskɛ: dra:gı]
fast train	rychlík (m)	[rıɦli:k]
diesel locomotive	motorová lokomotiva (f)	[motorova: lokomotıva]
steam engine	parní lokomotiva (f)	[parni: lokomotıva]
coach, carriage	vůz (m)	[vu:z]
restaurant car	jídelní vůz (m)	[jı:dɛlni: vu:z]
rails	koleje (f pl)	[kolɛje]
railway	železnice (f pl)	[ʒelɛznitse]
sleeper (track support)	pražec (m)	[praʒets]
platform (railway ~)	nástupiště (n)	[na:stupiʃte]
platform (~ 1, 2, etc.)	kolej (f)	[kolɛj]
semaphore	návěstidlo (n)	[na:vʰestidlo]
station	stanice (f)	[stanitse]
train driver	strojvůdce (m)	[strojvu:dtse]
porter (of luggage)	nosič (m)	[nositʃ]
train steward	průvodčí (m)	[pru:vodtʃi:]
passenger	cestující (m)	[tsestujı:tsi:]
ticket inspector	revizor (m)	[rɛwizor]
corridor (in train)	chodba (f)	[ɦodba]
emergency break	záchranná brzda (f)	[za:ɦrana: brzda]
compartment	oddělení (n)	[oddelɛni:]
berth	lůžko (n)	[lu:ʒko]
upper berth	horní lůžko (n)	[gorni: lu:ʒko]
lower berth	dolní lůžko (n)	[dolni: lu:ʒko]
linen	lůžkoviny (f pl)	[lu:ʒkowinı]
ticket	jízdenka (f)	[jı:zdɛŋka]
timetable	jízdní řád (m)	[jı:zdni: rʒa:d]
information display	tabule (f)	[tabulɛ]
to leave, to depart	odjíždět	[odʰjı:ʒdet]
departure (of train)	odjezd (m)	[odʰezd]
to arrive (ab. train)	přijíždět	[prʃijı:ʒdet]
arrival	příjezd (m)	[prʃi:jezd]
to arrive by train	přijet vlakem	[prʃijet vlakɛm]
to get on the train	nastoupit do vlaku	[nastoupit do vlaku]
to get off the train	vystoupit z vlaku	[vıstoupit z vlaku]
train crash	železniční neštěstí (n)	[ʒelɛznitʃni: nɛʃtesti:]
steam engine	parní lokomotiva (f)	[parni: lokomotıva]
stoker, fireman	topič (m)	[topitʃ]
firebox	topeniště (n)	[topɛniʃte]
coal	uhlí (n)	[ugli:]

107. Ship

| ship | loď (f) | [lodʲ] |
| vessel | loď (f) | [lodʲ] |

steamship	parník (m)	[parniːk]
riverboat	říční loď (f)	[riʧni lodʲ]
ocean liner	linková loď (f)	[liŋkovaː lodʲ]
cruiser	křižník (m)	[krʒiʒniːk]

yacht	jachta (f)	[jaɦta]
tugboat	vlek (m)	[vlɛk]
barge	vlečná nákladní loď (f)	[vlɛʧna: na:kladni: lodʲ]
ferry	prám (m)	[praːm]

| sailing ship | plachetnice (f) | [plaɦɛtniʦe] |
| brigantine | brigantina (f) | [brigantɪːna] |

| ice breaker | ledoborec (m) | [lɛdoborɛʦ] |
| submarine | ponorka (f) | [ponorka] |

boat (flat-bottomed ~)	loďka (f)	[lodʲka]
dinghy	člun (m)	[ʧlun]
lifeboat	záchranný člun (m)	[zaːɦranɪ ʧlun]
motorboat	motorový člun (m)	[motorovɪ ʧlun]

captain	kapitán (m)	[kapitaːn]
seaman	námořník (m)	[naːmorʒniːk]
sailor	námořník (m)	[naːmorʒniːk]
crew	posádka (f)	[posaːdka]

boatswain	loďmistr (m)	[lodʲmistr]
ship's boy	plavčík (m)	[plavʧiːk]
cook	lodní kuchař (m)	[lodni: kuɦarʒ]
ship's doctor	lodní lékař (m)	[lodni: lɛːkarʒ]

deck	paluba (f)	[paluba]
mast	stěžeň (m)	[stɛʒeɲ]
sail	plachta (f)	[plaɦta]

hold	podpalubí (n)	[podpalubiː]
bow (prow)	příď (f)	[prʃiːdʲ]
stern	záď (f)	[zaːdʲ]
oar	veslo (n)	[vɛslo]
propeller	šroub (m)	[ʃroub]

cabin	kajuta (f)	[kajuta]
wardroom	společenská místnost (f)	[spolɛʧenska: miːstnost]
engine room	strojovna (f)	[strojovna]
the bridge	kapitánský můstek (m)	[kapitaːnskɪ muːstɛk]
radio room	rádiová kabina (f)	[ra:dɪjova kabina]
wave (radio)	vlna (f)	[vlna]
logbook	lodní deník (m)	[lodni: dɛniːk]
spyglass	dalekohled (m)	[dalɛkogled]
bell	zvon (m)	[zvon]

flag	vlajka (f)	[vlajka]
rope (mooring ~)	lano (n)	[lano]
knot (bowline, etc.)	uzel (m)	[uzɛl]

| handrail | zábradlí (n) | [zaːbradliː] |
| gangway | schůdky (m pl) | [sɦuːdkɪ] |

anchor	kotva (f)	[kotva]
to weigh anchor	zvednout kotvy	[zvɛdnout kotvɪ]
to drop anchor	spustit kotvy	[spustit kotvɪ]
anchor chain	kotevní řetěz (m)	[kotɛvniː rʒetez]

port (harbour)	přístav (m)	[prʃiːstav]
wharf, quay	přístaviště (n)	[prʃiːstawiʃte]
to berth (moor)	přistávat	[prʃistaːvat]
to cast off	vyplouvat	[vɪplouvat]

trip, voyage	cestování (n)	[tsestovaːniː]
cruise (sea trip)	plavba (f) po turistické trase	[plavba po turistɪtskeː trasɛ]
course (route)	kurz (m)	[kurz]
route (itinerary)	trasa (f)	[trasa]

fairway	plavební dráha (f)	[plavɛbniː draːga]
shallows (shoal)	mělčina (f)	[mneltʃina]
to run aground	najet na mělčinu	[najet na mneltʃinu]

storm	bouřka (f)	[bourʒka]
signal	signál (m)	[signaːl]
to sink (vi)	potápět se	[potaːpʰet sɛ]
SOS	SOS	[ɛs oː ɛs]
ring buoy	záchranný kruh (m)	[zaːɦranɪ kruɦ]

108. Airport

airport	letiště (n)	[lɛtiʃte]
aeroplane	letadlo (n)	[lɛtadlo]
airline	letecká společnost (f)	[lɛtɛtska: spolɛtʃnost]
air-traffic controller	dispečer (m)	[dispɛtʃer]

departure	odlet (m)	[odlɛt]
arrival	přílet (m)	[prʃiːlɛt]
to arrive (by plane)	přiletět	[prʃilɛtet]

| departure time | čas (m) odletu | [tʃas odlɛtu] |
| arrival time | čas (m) příletu (m) | [tʃas prʃilɛtu] |

| to be delayed | mít zpoždění | [miːt spoʒdɛni] |
| flight delay | zpoždění (n) odletu | [spoʒdeni: odlɛtu] |

information board	informační tabule (f)	[informatʃni: tabulɛ]
information	informace (f)	[informatse]
to announce (vt)	hlásit	[glaːsit]
flight (e.g. next ~)	let (m)	[lɛt]
customs	celnice (f)	[tselnitse]

customs officer	celník (m)	[ʦelni:k]
customs declaration	prohlášení (n)	[progla:ʃɛni:]
to fill in the declaration	vyplnit prohlášení	[vɪplnit progla:ʃɛni:]
passport control	pasová kontrola (f)	[pasova: kontrola]

luggage	zavazadla (n pl)	[zavazadla]
hand luggage	příruční zavazadlo (n)	[prʃi:ruʧni: zavazadlo]
Lost Luggage Desk	hledání (n) zavazadel	[glɛda:ni: zavazadɛl]
luggage trolley	vozík (m) na zavazadla	[vozi:k na zavazadla]

landing	přistání (n)	[prʃista:ni:]
landing strip	přistávací dráha (f)	[prʃista:vaʦi: dra:ga]
to land (vi)	přistávat	[prʃista:vat]
airstairs	pojízdné schůdky (m pl)	[pojɪ:zdnɛ: sɦu:dkɪ]

check-in	registrace (f)	[rɛgistraʦe]
check-in desk	přepážka (f) registrace	[prʃɛpa:ʒka rɛgistraʦe]
to check-in (vi)	zaregistrovat se	[zarɛgistrovat sɛ]
boarding pass	palubní lístek (m)	[palubni: li:stɛk]
departure gate	příchod (m) k nástupu	[prʃi:ɦod k na:stupu]

transit	tranzit (m)	[tranzit]
to wait (vt)	čekat	[ʧekat]
departure lounge	čekárna (f)	[ʧeka:rna]
to see off	doprovázet	[doprova:zɛt]
to say goodbye	loučit se	[louʧit sɛ]

Life events

109. Holidays. Event

celebration, holiday	svátek (m)	[sva:tɛk]
national day	národní svátek (m)	[na:rodni: sva:tɛk]
public holiday	sváteční den (m)	[sva:tɛtʃni: dɛn]
to fete (celebrate)	oslavovat	[oslavovat]
event (happening)	událost (f)	[uda:lost]
event (organized activity)	akce (f)	[aktse]
banquet (party)	banket (m)	[baŋkɛt]
reception (formal party)	recepce (f)	[rɛtseptse]
feast	hostina (f)	[gostina]
anniversary	výročí (n)	[vɪ:rotʃi:]
jubilee	jubileum (n)	[jubilɛjum]
to celebrate (vt)	oslavit	[oslawit]
New Year	Nový rok (m)	[novɪ: rok]
Happy New Year!	Šťastný nový rok!	[ʃtʲastnɪ: novɪ: rok]
Christmas	Vánoce (f pl)	[va:notse]
Merry Christmas!	Veselé vánoce!	[vɛsɛlɛ: va:notse]
Christmas tree	vánoční stromek (m)	[va:notʃni: stromɛk]
fireworks	ohňostroj (m)	[ognɜstroj]
wedding	svatba (f)	[svatba]
groom	ženich (m)	[ʒeniɦ]
bride	nevěsta (f)	[nɛvʰesta]
to invite (vt)	zvát	[zva:t]
invitation card	pozvánka (f)	[pozva:ŋka]
guest	host (m)	[gost]
to visit (go to see)	jít na návštěvu	[jɪ:t na na:vʃtevu]
to greet the guests	vítat hosty	[witat gosti:]
gift, present	dárek (m)	[da:rɛk]
to give (sth as present)	darovat	[darovat]
to receive gifts	dostávat dárky	[dosta:vat da:rkɪ]
bouquet (of flowers)	kytice (f)	[kɪtitse]
greetings (New Year ~)	blahopřání (n)	[blagoprʃa:ni:]
to congratulate (vt)	blahopřát	[blagoprʃa:t]
greetings card	blahopřejný lístek (m)	[blagoprʃɛjnɪ: li:stɛk]
to send a postcard	poslat lístek	[poslat li:stɛk]
to get a postcard	dostat lístek	[dostat li:stɛk]
toast	přípitek (m)	[prʃi:pitɛk]

| to offer (a drink, etc.) | častovat | [tʃastovat] |
| champagne | šampaňské (n) | [ʃampaɲskɛ:] |

to have fun	bavit se	[bawit sɛ]
fun, merriment	zábava (f)	[za:bava]
joy (emotion)	radost (f)	[radost]

| dance | tanec (m) | [tanɛts] |
| to dance (vi, vt) | tančit | [tantʃit] |

| waltz | valčík (m) | [valtʃi:k] |
| tango | tango (n) | [taŋo] |

110. Funerals. Burial

cemetery	hřbitov (m)	[grʒbitov]
grave, tomb	hrob (m)	[grob]
cross	kříž (m)	[krʃi:ʒ]
gravestone	náhrobek (m)	[na:grobɛk]
fence	ohrádka (f)	[ogra:dka]
chapel	kaple (f)	[kaplɛ]

death	úmrtí (n)	[u:mrti:]
to die (vi)	umřít	[umrʒi:t]
the deceased	zemřelý (m)	[zɛmrʒelı:]
mourning	smutek (m)	[smutɛk]

to bury (vt)	pohřbívat	[pogrʒbi:vat]
undertakers	pohřební ústav (m)	[pogrʒebni: u:stav]
funeral	pohřeb (m)	[pogrʒeb]

wreath	věnec (m)	[vʰenɛts]
coffin	rakev (f)	[rakɛv]
hearse	katafalk (m)	[katafalk]
shroud	pohřební roucho (m)	[pogrʒebni: rouɦo]

| cremation urn | popelnice (f) | [popɛlnitse] |
| crematorium | krematorium (n) | [krɛmatorijum] |

obituary	nekrolog (m)	[nɛkrolog]
to cry (weep)	plakat	[plakat]
to sob (vi)	vzlykat	[vzlıkat]

111. War. Soldiers

platoon	četa (f)	[tʃeta]
company	rota (f)	[rota]
regiment	pluk (m)	[pluk]
army	armáda (f)	[arma:da]
division	divize (f)	[diwizɛ]
detachment	oddíl (m)	[oddi:l]
host (army)	vojsko (n)	[vojsko]

| soldier | voják (m) | [voja:k] |
| officer | důstojník (m) | [du:stojni:k] |

private	vojín (m)	[vojɪ:n]
sergeant	seržant (m)	[sɛrʒant]
lieutenant	poručík (m)	[porutʃi:k]
captain	kapitán (m)	[kapita:n]
major	major (m)	[major]
colonel	plukovník (m)	[plukovni:k]
general	generál (m)	[gɛnɛra:l]

sailor	námořník (m)	[na:morʒni:k]
captain	kapitán (m)	[kapita:n]
boatswain	loďmistr (m)	[loďmistr]

artilleryman	dělostřelec (m)	[delostrʃɛlɛts]
paratrooper	výsadkář (m)	[vɪ:sadka:rʒ]
pilot	letec (m)	[lɛtɛts]
navigator	navigátor (m)	[nawiga:tor]
mechanic	mechanik (m)	[mɛɦanɪk]

pioneer (sapper)	ženista (m)	[ʒenɪsta]
parachutist	parašutista (m)	[paraʃutista]
scout	rozvědčík (m)	[rozvʰedtʃi:k]
sniper	odstřelovač (m)	[odstrʃɛlovatʃ]

patrol (group)	hlídka (f)	[gli:dka]
to patrol (vt)	hlídkovat	[gli:dkovat]
sentry, guard	strážný (m)	[stra:ʒnɪ:]

warrior	vojín (m)	[vojɪ:n]
hero	hrdina (m)	[grdina]
heroine	hrdinka (f)	[grdiŋka]
patriot	vlastenec (m)	[vlastɛnɛts]

traitor	zrádce (m)	[zra:dtse]
deserter	zběh (m)	[zbʰeɦ]
to desert (vi)	dezertovat	[dɛzɛrtovat]

mercenary	žoldnéř (m)	[ʒoldnɛ:rʒ]
recruit	branec (m)	[branɛts]
volunteer	dobrovolník (m)	[dobrovolni:k]

dead	zabitý (m)	[zabitɪ:]
wounded (n)	raněný (m)	[ranenɪ:]
prisoner of war	zajatec (m)	[zajatɛts]

112. War. Military actions. Part 1

war	válka (f)	[va:lka]
to be at war	bojovat	[bojovat]
civil war	občanská válka (f)	[obtʃanska: va:lka]
treacherously (adv)	věrolomně	[vʰerolomne]
declaration of war	vyhlášení (n)	[vɪgla:ʃɛni:]

to declare (~ war)	vyhlásit	[vɪgla:sit]
aggression	agrese (f)	[agrɛsɛ]
to attack (invade)	přepadat	[prʃɛpadat]

to invade (vt)	uchvacovat	[uɦvaʦovat]
invader	uchvatitel (m)	[uɦvatitɛl]
conqueror	dobyvatel (m)	[dobɪvatɛl]

defence	obrana (f)	[obrana]
to defend (a country, etc.)	bránit	[bra:nit]
to defend oneself	bránit se	[bra:nit sɛ]

| enemy, adversary | nepřítel (m) | [nɛprʃi:tɛl] |
| enemy (as adj) | nepřátelský | [nɛprʃa:tɛlskɪ:] |

| strategy | strategie (f) | [stratɛgije] |
| tactics | taktika (f) | [taktɪka] |

order	rozkaz (m)	[rozkaz]
command (order)	povel (m)	[povɛl]
to order (vt)	rozkazovat	[rozkazovat]
mission	úkol (m)	[u:kol]
secret (adj)	tajný	[tajnɪ:]

| battle | bitva (f) | [bitva] |
| combat | boj (m) | [boj] |

attack	útok (m)	[u:tok]
storming (assault)	útok (m)	[u:tok]
to storm (vt)	dobývat útokem	[dobɪ:vat u:tokɛm]
siege (to be under ~)	obležení (n)	[oblɛʒeni:]

| offensive (n) | útok (m) | [u:tok] |
| to go on the offensive | útočit | [u:toʧit] |

| retreat | ústup (m) | [u:stup] |
| to retreat (vi) | ustupovat | [ustupovat] |

| encirclement | obklíčení (n) | [obkli:ʧeni:] |
| to encircle (vt) | obkličovat | [obkliʧovat] |

bombing (by aircraft)	bombardování (m)	[bombardova:ni:]
to drop a bomb	shodit pumu	[sɦodit pumu]
to bomb (vt)	bombardovat	[bombardovat]
explosion	výbuch (m)	[vɪ:buɦ]

shot	výstřel (m)	[vɪ:strʃɛl]
to fire a shot	vystřelit	[vɪstrʒelit]
shooting	střelba (f)	[strʃɛlba]

to take aim (at …)	mířit	[mi:rʒit]
to point (a gun)	zamířit	[zami:rʒit]
to hit (the target)	zasáhnout	[zasa:gnout]

| to sink (~ a ship) | potopit | [potopit] |
| hole (in a ship) | trhlina (f) | [trglina] |

to founder, to sink (vi)	topit se	[topit sɛ]
front (at war)	fronta (f)	[fronta]
rear (homefront)	týl (m)	[tɪːl]
evacuation	evakuace (f)	[ɛvakuatse]
to evacuate (vt)	evakuovat	[ɛvakuovat]

barbed wire	ostnatý drát (m)	[ostnatɪ: draːt]
barrier (anti tank ~)	zátaras (m)	[zaːtaras]
watchtower	věž (f)	[vʰeʒ]

hospital	vojenská nemocnice (f)	[vojenska: nɛmotsnitse]
to wound (vt)	zranit	[zranit]
wound	rána (f)	[raːna]
wounded (n)	raněný (m)	[ranenɪː]
to be injured	utrpět zranění	[utrpʰet zraneni:]
serious (wound)	těžký	[teʒkɪː]

113. War. Military actions. Part 2

captivity	zajetí (n)	[zajeti:]
to take captive	zajmout	[zajmout]
to be in captivity	být v zajetí	[bɪːt v zajeti:]
to be taken prisoner	dostat se do zajetí	[dostat sɛ do zajeti:]

concentration camp	koncentrační tábor (m)	[kontsentratʃni: taːbor]
prisoner of war	zajatec (m)	[zajatɛts]
to escape (vi)	utéci	[utɛːtsi]

to betray (vt)	zradit	[zradit]
betrayer	zrádce (m)	[zraːdtse]
betrayal	zrada (f)	[zrada]

| to execute (shoot) | zastřelit | [zastrʃɛlit] |
| execution (shooting) | smrt (f) zastřelením | [smrt zastrʃɛlɛni:m] |

equipment (uniform, etc.)	výstroj (f)	[vɪːstroj]
shoulder board	náramenik (m)	[na:ramɛni:k]
gas mask	plynová maska (f)	[plɪnova: maska]

radio transmitter	vysílačka (f)	[vɪsi:latʃka]
cipher, code	šifra (f)	[ʃifra]
conspiracy	konspirace (f)	[konspiratse]
password	heslo (n)	[gɛslo]

land mine	mina (f)	[mina]
to mine (road, etc.)	zaminovat	[zaminovat]
minefield	minové pole (n)	[minove: polɛ]

| air-raid warning | letecký poplach (m) | [lɛtɛtskɪ: poplaɦ] |
| alarm (warning) | poplach (m) | [poplaɦ] |

signal	signál (m)	[signa:l]
signal flare	světlice (f)	[svʰetlitse]
headquarters	štáb (m)	[ʃta:b]

reconnaissance	rozvědka (f)	[rozvʰedka]
situation	situace (f)	[situatse]
report	hlášení (n)	[gla:ʃɛni:]
ambush	záloha (f)	[za:loga]
reinforcement (of army)	posila (f)	[posila]

target	terč (m)	[tɛrtʃ]
training area	střelnice (f)	[strʃɛlnitse]
military exercise	manévry (m pl)	[manɛ:vrɪ]

panic	panika (f)	[panɪka]
devastation	rozvrat (m)	[rozvrat]
destruction, ruins	zpustošení (n)	[spustoʃɛni:]
to destroy (vt)	zpustošit	[spustoʃit]

to survive (vi, vt)	přežít	[prʃɛʒi:t]
to disarm (vt)	odzbrojit	[odzbrojɪt]
to handle (~ a gun)	zacházet	[zaɦa:zɛt]

Attention!	Pozor!	[pozor]
At ease!	Pohov!	[pogov]

feat (of courage)	hrdinský čin (m)	[grdinskɪ: tʃin]
oath (vow)	přísaha (f)	[prʃi:saga]
to swear (an oath)	přísahat	[prʃi:sagat]

decoration (medal, etc.)	vyznamenání (n)	[vɪznamɛna:ni:]
to award (give medal to)	vyznamenávat	[vɪznamɛna:vat]
medal	medaile (f)	[mɛdajlɛ]
order (e.g. ~ of Merit)	řád (m)	[rʒa:d]

victory	vítězství (n)	[wi:tezstwi:]
defeat	porážka (f)	[pora:ʒka]
armistice	příměří (n)	[prʃi:mnerʒi:]

banner (flag)	prapor (m)	[prapor]
glory (honour, fame)	sláva (f)	[sla:va]
parade	vojenská přehlídka (f)	[vojenska: prʃɛgli:dka]
to march (on parade)	pochodovat	[poɦodovat]

114. Weapons

weapons	zbraň (f)	[zbraɲ]
firearm	střelná zbraň (f)	[strʃɛlna: zbraɲ]
cold weapons (knives, etc.)	bodná a sečná zbraň (f)	[bodna: a sɛtʃna: zbraɲ]

chemical weapons	chemická zbraň (f)	[ɦɛmitska: zbraɲ]
nuclear (adj)	jaderný	[jadɛrnɪ:]
nuclear weapons	jaderná zbraň (f)	[jadɛrna: zbraɲ]
bomb	puma (f)	[puma]
atomic bomb	atomová puma (f)	[atomova: puma]

pistol (gun)	pistole (f)	[pistolɛ]
rifle	puška (f)	[puʃka]

| submachine gun | samopal (m) | [samopal] |
| machine gun | kulomet (m) | [kulomɛt] |

muzzle	ústí (n) hlavně	[uːsti: glavne]
barrel	hlaveň (f)	[glavɛɲ]
calibre	ráž (f)	[raːʒ]

trigger	kohoutek (m)	[kogoutɛk]
sight (aiming device)	hledí (n)	[glɛdiː]
magazine	zásobník (m)	[zaːsobniːk]
butt (of rifle)	pažba (f)	[paʒba]

| hand grenade | granát (m) | [granaːt] |
| explosive | výbušnina (f) | [vɪːbuʃnina] |

| bullet | kulka (f) | [kulka] |
| cartridge | náboj (m) | [naːboj] |

| charge | nálož (f) | [naːloʒ] |
| ammunition | střelivo (n) | [strʃɛlivo] |

bomber (aircraft)	bombardér (m)	[bombardɛːr]
fighter	stíhačka (f)	[stiːgatʃka]
helicopter	vrtulník (m)	[vrtulniːk]

anti-aircraft gun	protiletadlové dělo (n)	[protilɛtadlovɛː delo]
tank	tank (m)	[taŋk]
tank gun	tankové dělo (n)	[taŋkovɛː delo]

artillery	dělostřelectvo (n)	[delostrʃɛlɛtstvo]
cannon	dělo (n)	[delo]
to lay (a gun)	zamířit	[zamiːrʒit]

shell (projectile)	střela (f)	[strʃɛla]
mortar bomb	mina (f)	[mina]
mortar	minomet (m)	[minomɛt]
splinter (of shell)	střepina (f)	[strʃɛpina]

submarine	ponorka (f)	[ponorka]
torpedo	torpédo (n)	[torpɛːdo]
missile	raketa (f)	[rakɛta]

to load (gun)	nabíjet	[nabiːjet]
to shoot (vi)	střílet	[strʃiːlɛt]
to take aim (at ...)	mířit	[miːrʒit]
bayonet	bodák (m)	[bodaːk]

epee	kord (m)	[kord]
sabre (e.g. cavalry ~)	šavle (f)	[ʃavlɛ]
spear (weapon)	kopí (n)	[kopiː]

| bow | luk (m) | [luk] |
| arrow | šíp (m) | [ʃiːp] |

| musket | mušketa (f) | [muʃkɛta] |
| crossbow | samostříl (m) | [samostrʃiːl] |

115. Ancient people

primitive (prehistoric)	prvobytný	[prvobɪtnɪ:]
prehistoric (adj)	prehistorický	[prɛgistoritskɪ:]
ancient (~ civilization)	starobylý	[starobɪlɪ:]
Stone Age	doba (f) kamenná	[doba kamɛna:]
Bronze Age	doba (f) bronzová	[doba bronzova:]
Ice Age	doba (f) ledová	[doba lɛdova:]
tribe	kmen (m)	[kmɛn]
cannibal	lidojed (m)	[lidojed]
hunter	lovec (m)	[lovɛʦ]
to hunt (vi, vt)	lovit	[lowit]
mammoth	mamut (m)	[mamut]
cave	jeskyně (f)	[jeskɪne]
fire	oheň (m)	[ogɛɲ]
campfire	táborák (m)	[taborak]
rock painting	jeskynní malba (f)	[jeskɪni: malba]
tool (e.g. stone axe)	pracovní nástroje (m pl)	[praʦovni: na:stroje]
spear	oštěp (m)	[oʃtep]
stone axe	kamenná sekera (f)	[kamɛna: sɛkɛra]
to be at war	bojovat	[bojovat]
to domesticate (vt)	ochočovat	[ohoʧovat]
idol	modla (f)	[modla]
to worship (vt)	klanět se	[klanet sɛ]
superstition	pověra (f)	[povʰera]
evolution	evoluce (f)	[ɛvoluʦɛ]
development	rozvoj (m)	[rozvoj]
disappearance	vymizení (n)	[vɪmizɛni:]
to adapt oneself	přizpůsobovat se	[prʃispu:sobovatsɛ]
archaeology	archeologie (f)	[arɦɛologiɛ]
archaeologist	archeolog (m)	[arɦɛolog]
archaeological (adj)	archeologický	[arɦɛologitskɪ:]
excavation site	vykopávky (f pl)	[vɪkopa:vkɪ]
excavations	vykopávky (f pl)	[vɪkopa:vkɪ]
find (object)	objev (m)	[obʰef]
fragment	část (f)	[ʧa:st]

116. Middle Ages

people (population)	lid (m)	[lid]
peoples	národy (m pl)	[na:rodɪ]
tribe	kmen (m)	[kmɛn]
tribes	kmeny (m pl)	[kmɛni]
barbarians	barbaři (m pl)	[barbarʒi]
Gauls	Galové (m pl)	[galovɛ:]

Goths	Gótové (m pl)	[go:tovɛ:]
Slavs	Slované (m pl)	[slovanɛ:]
Vikings	Vikingové (m pl)	[vɪkiɲovɛ:]

| Romans | Římané (m pl) | [rʒi:manɛ:] |
| Roman (adj) | římský | [rʒi:mskɪ:] |

Byzantines	obyvatelé (m pl)	[obɪvatɛlɛ:
	Byzantské říše (f)	bɪzantskɛ: rʃi:ʃɛ]
Byzantium	Byzantská říše (f)	[bɪzantska: rʃi:ʃɛ]
Byzantine (adj)	byzantský	[bɪzantskɪ:]

emperor	císař (m)	[tsi:sarʒ]
leader, chief	vůdce (m)	[vu:dtsɛ]
powerful (~ king)	mocný	[motsnɪ:]
king	král (m)	[kra:l]
ruler (sovereign)	vladař (m)	[vladarʒ]

knight	rytíř (m)	[rɪti:rʒ]
knightly (adj)	rytířský	[rɪti:rʃskɪ:]
feudal lord	feudál (m)	[fɛuda:l]
feudal (adj)	feudální	[fɛuda:lni:]
vassal	vasal (m)	[vasal]

duke	vévoda (m)	[vɛ:voda]
earl	hrabě (m)	[grabe]
baron	barel (m)	[barɛl]
bishop	biskup (m)	[biskup]

armour	brnění (n)	[brneni:]
shield	štít (m)	[ʃti:t]
sword	meč (m)	[mɛtʃ]
visor	hledí (n)	[glɛdi:]
chain armour	kroužková košile (f)	[krouʒkova: koʃilɛ]

| crusade | křižácká výprava (f) | [krʃiʒa:tska: vɪ:prava] |
| crusader | křižák (m) | [krʃiʒa:k] |

territory	území (n)	[u:zɛmi:]
to attack (invade)	přepadat	[prʃɛpadat]
to conquer (vt)	dobýt	[dobɪ:t]
to occupy (invade)	zmocnit se	[zmotsnitsɛ]

siege (to be under ~)	obležení (n)	[oblɛʒeni:]
besieged (adj)	obklíčený	[obkli:tʃenu:]
to besiege (vt)	obklíčovat	[obklitʃovat]

inquisition	inkvizice (f)	[iɲkwizitsɛ]
inquisitor	inkvizitor (m)	[iɲkwizitor]
torture	mučení (n)	[mutʃeni:]
cruel (adj)	krutý	[krutɪ:]
heretic	kacíř (m)	[katsi:rʒ]
heresy	bludařství (n)	[bludarʃstwi:]

| seafaring | mořeplavba (f) | [morʒeplavba] |
| pirate | pirát (m) | [pira:t] |

piracy	pirátství (n)	[piraːʦwiː]
boarding (attack)	abordáž (f)	[abordaːʒ]
loot, booty	kořist (f)	[korʒist]
treasures	bohatství (n)	[bogaʦwiː]

discovery	objevení (n)	[obʰevɛniː]
to discover (new land, etc.)	objevit	[obʰewit]
expedition	výprava (f)	[vɪːprava]

musketeer	mušketýr (m)	[muʃkɛtːɪr]
cardinal	kardinál (m)	[kardinaːl]
heraldry	heraldika (f)	[gɛraldika]
heraldic (adj)	heraldický	[gɛralditskɪː]

117. Leader. Chief. Authorities

king	král (m)	[kraːl]
queen	královna (f)	[kraːlovna]
royal (adj)	královský	[kraːlovskɪː]
kingdom	království (n)	[kraːlovstwiː]

| prince | princ (m) | [prinʦ] |
| princess | princezna (f) | [prinʦezna] |

president	prezident (m)	[prɛzidɛnt]
vice-president	viceprezident (m)	[witseprɛzidɛnt]
senator	senátor (m)	[sɛnaːtor]

monarch	monarcha (m)	[monarɦa]
ruler (sovereign)	vladař (m)	[vladarʒ]
dictator	diktátor (m)	[dɪktaːtor]
tyrant	tyran (m)	[tɪran]
magnate	magnát (m)	[magnaːt]

director	ředitel (m)	[rʒeditɛl]
chief	šéf (m)	[ʃɛːf]
manager (director)	správce (m)	[spraːvʦe]
boss	bos (m)	[bos]
owner	majitel (m)	[majɪtɛl]

head (~ of delegation)	hlava (m)	[glava]
authorities	úřady (m pl)	[uːrʒadɪ]
superiors	vedení (n)	[vɛdɛniː]

governor	gubernátor (m)	[gubɛrnaːtor]
consul	konzul (m)	[konzul]
diplomat	diplomat (m)	[dɪplomat]
mayor	primátor (m)	[primaːtor]
sheriff	šerif (m)	[ʃɛrif]

emperor	císař (m)	[ʦiːsarʒ]
tsar, czar	car (m)	[ʦar]
Pharaoh	faraón (m)	[faraoːn]
khan	chán (m)	[ɦaːn]

118. Breaking the law. Criminals. Part 1

bandit	bandita (m)	[bandɪta]
crime	zločin (m)	[zlotʃin]
criminal (person)	zločinec (m)	[zlotʃinɛts]
thief	zloděj (m)	[zlodej]
to steal (vi, vt)	krást	[kra:st]
stealing (larceny)	loupež (f)	[loupɛʒ]
theft	krádež (f)	[kra:dɛʒ]
to kidnap (vt)	unést	[unɛ:st]
kidnapping	únos (m)	[u:nos]
kidnapper	únosce (m)	[u:nostse]
ransom	výkupné (n)	[vɪ:kupnɛ:]
to demand ransom	žádat výkupné	[ʒa:dat vɪ:kupnɛ:]
to rob (vt)	loupit	[loupit]
robbery	loupež (f)	[loupɛʒ]
robber	lupič (m)	[lupitʃ]
to extort (vt)	vydírat	[vɪdi:rat]
extortionist	vyděrač (m)	[vɪderatʃ]
extortion	vyděračství (n)	[vɪderatʃstwi:]
to murder, to kill	zabít	[zabi:t]
murder	vražda (f)	[vraʒda]
murderer	vrah (m)	[vraɦ]
gunshot	výstřel (m)	[vɪ:strʃɛl]
to fire a shot	vystřelit	[vɪstrʒelit]
to shoot down	zastřelit	[zastrʃɛlit]
to shoot (vi)	střílet	[strʃi:lɛt]
shooting	střelba (f)	[strʃɛlba]
incident (fight, etc.)	nehoda (f)	[nɛgoda]
fight, brawl	rvačka (f)	[rvatʃka]
Help!	Pomoc!	[pomots]
victim	oběť (f)	[obʰetʲ]
to damage (vt)	poškodit	[poʃkodit]
damage	škoda (f)	[ʃkoda]
dead body	mrtvola (f)	[mrtvola]
grave (~ crime)	těžký	[teʒkɪ:]
to attack (vt)	napadnout	[napadnout]
to beat (dog, person)	bít	[bi:t]
to beat up	zbít	[zbi:t]
to take (snatch)	odebrat	[odɛbrat]
to stab to death	zabít	[zabi:t]
to maim (vt)	zmrzačit	[zmrzatʃit]
to wound (vt)	zranit	[zranit]
blackmail	vyděračství (n)	[vɪderatʃstwi:]
to blackmail (vt)	vydírat	[vɪdi:rat]

blackmailer	vyděrač (m)	[vɪderatʃ]
protection racket	vyděračství (n)	[vɪderatʃstwiː]
racketeer	vyděrač (m)	[vɪderatʃ]
gangster	gangster (m)	[gaŋstɛr]
mafia	mafie (f)	[mafije]

pickpocket	kapsář (m)	[kapsaːrʒ]
burglar	kasař (m)	[kasarʒ]
smuggling	pašování (n)	[paʃovaːniː]
smuggler	pašerák (m)	[paʃɛraːk]

forgery	padělání (n)	[padelaːniː]
to forge (counterfeit)	padělat	[padelat]
fake (forged)	padělaný	[padelanɪː]

119. Breaking the law. Criminals. Part 2

rape	znásilnění (n)	[znaːsilneni:]
to rape (vt)	znásilnit	[znaːsilnit]
rapist	násilník (m)	[naːsilniːk]
maniac	maniak (m)	[manɪjak]

prostitute (fem.)	prostitutka (f)	[prostɪtutka]
prostitution	prostituce (f)	[prostɪtutse]
pimp	kuplíř (m)	[kupliːrʒ]

drug addict	narkoman (m)	[narkoman]
drug dealer	drogový dealer (m)	[drogovɪ diːlɛr]

to blow up (bomb)	vyhodit do povětří	[vɪgodit do povʰetrʃi:]
explosion	výbuch (m)	[vɪːbuɦ]
to set fire	zapálit	[zapaːlit]
incendiary (arsonist)	žhář (m)	[ʒgaːrʒ]

terrorism	terorismus (m)	[tɛrorizmus]
terrorist	terorista (m)	[tɛrorista]
hostage	rukojmí (m)	[rukojmi:]

to swindle (vt)	oklamat	[oklamat]
swindle	podvod (m)	[podvod]
swindler	podvodník (m)	[podvodni:k]

to bribe (vt)	podplatit	[podplatit]
bribery	podplácení (n)	[podplaːtseni:]
bribe	úplatek (m)	[u:platɛk]

poison	jed (m)	[jed]
to poison (vt)	otrávit	[otraːwit]
to poison oneself	otrávit se	[otraːwit sɛ]

suicide (act)	sebevražda (f)	[sɛbɛvraʒda]
suicide (person)	sebevrah (m)	[sɛbɛvraɦ]
to threaten (vt)	vyhrožovat	[vɪgroʒovat]
threat	vyhrůžka (f)	[vɪgruːʒka]

| to make an attempt | páchat atentát | [pa:ɦat atenta:t] |
| attempt (attack) | atentát (m) | [atɛnta:t] |

| to steal (a car) | unést | [unɛ:st] |
| to hijack (a plane) | unést | [unɛ:st] |

| revenge | pomsta (f) | [pomsta] |
| to avenge (vt) | mstít se | [msti:t sɛ] |

to torture (vt)	mučit	[mutʃit]
torture	mučení (n)	[mutʃeni:]
to abuse (treat cruelly)	trápit	[tra:pit]

pirate	pirát (m)	[pira:t]
hooligan	chuligán (m)	[ɦuliga:n]
armed (adj)	ozbrojený	[ozbrojenɪ:]
violence	násilí (n)	[na:sili:]

| spying (n) | špionáž (f) | [ʃpijona:ʒ] |
| to spy (vi) | špehovat | [ʃpɛgovat] |

120. Police. Law. Part 1

| justice | soud (m) | [soud] |
| court (court room) | soud (m) | [soud] |

judge	soudce (m)	[soudtse]
jurors	porotci (m pl)	[porottsi]
jury trial	porota (f)	[porota]
to judge (vt)	soudit	[soudit]

lawyer, barrister	advokát (m)	[advoka:t]
accused	obžalovaný (m)	[obʒalovanɪ:]
dock	lavice (f) obžalovaných	[lawitse obʒalovanɪ:ɦ]

| charge | žaloba (f) | [ʒaloba] |
| accused | obžalovaný (m) | [obʒalovanɪ:] |

| sentence | rozsudek (m) | [rozsudɛk] |
| to sentence (vt) | odsoudit | [odsoudit] |

guilty (culprit)	viník (m)	[wini:k]
to punish (vt)	potrestat	[potrɛstat]
punishment	trest (m)	[trɛst]

fine (penalty)	pokuta (f)	[pokuta]
life imprisonment	doživotní vězení (n)	[doʒivotni: vʰezɛni:]
death penalty	trest (m) smrti	[trɛst smrti]
electric chair	elektrické křeslo (n)	[ɛlɛktritskɛ: krʃɛslo]
gallows	šibenice (f)	[ʃibɛnitse]

to execute (vt)	popravit	[poprawit]
execution	poprava (f)	[poprava]
prison, jail	vězení (n)	[vʰezɛni:]

cell	**cela** (f)	[ʦela]
escort	**ozbrojený doprovod** (m)	[ozbrojenɪ doprovod]
prison officer	**dozorce** (m)	[dozorʦe]
prisoner	**vězeň** (m)	[vʰezɛɲ]

handcuffs	**pouta** (n pl)	[pouta]
to handcuff (vt)	**nasadit pouta**	[nasadit pouta]

prison break	**útěk** (m)	[u:tek]
to break out (vi)	**uprchnout**	[uprɦnout]
to disappear (vi)	**zmizet**	[zmizɛt]
to release (from prison)	**propustit**	[propustit]
amnesty	**amnestie** (f)	[amnɛstɪje]

police	**policie** (f)	[polɪʦije]
policeman	**policista** (m)	[polɪʦista]
police station	**policejní stanice** (f)	[polɪʦejni: stanɪʦe]
truncheon	**gumový obušek** (m)	[gumovɪ: obuʃɛk]
loudspeaker	**hlásná trouba** (f)	[gla:sna: trouba]

patrol car	**policejní vůz** (m)	[polɪʦejni: vu:z]
siren	**houkačka** (f)	[goukaʧka]
to turn on the siren	**zapnout houkačku**	[zapnout goukaʧku]
siren call	**houkání** (n)	[gouka:ni:]

scene of the crime	**místo** (n) **činu**	[mi:sto ʧinu]
witness	**svědek** (m)	[svʰedɛk]
freedom	**svoboda** (f)	[svoboda]
accomplice	**spolupachatel** (m)	[spolupaɦatɛl]
to flee (vi)	**zmizet**	[zmizɛt]
trace (to leave a ~)	**stopa** (f)	[stopa]

121. Police. Law. Part 2

search (for a criminal)	**pátrání** (n)	[pa:tra:ni:]
to look for ...	**pátrat**	[pa:trat]
suspicion	**podezření** (n)	[podɛzrʒeni:]
suspicious (suspect)	**podezřelý**	[podɛzrʒelɪ:]
to stop (cause to halt)	**zastavit**	[zastawit]
to detain (keep in custody)	**zadržet**	[zadrʒet]

case (lawsuit)	**případ** (m)	[prʃi:pad]
investigation	**vyšetřování** (n)	[vɪʃetrʃova:ni:]
detective	**detektiv** (m)	[dɛtɛktɪv]
investigator	**vyšetřovatel** (m)	[vɪʃetrʃovatɛl]
version	**verze** (f)	[vɛrzɛ]

motive	**motiv** (m)	[motɪv]
interrogation	**výslech** (m)	[vɪ:slɛɦ]
to interrogate (vt)	**vyslýchat**	[vɪslɪ:ɦat]
to question (vt)	**vyslýchat**	[vɪslɪ:ɦat]
checking (police ~)	**kontrola** (f)	[kontrola]
round-up	**zátah** (m)	[za:taɦ]
search (~ warrant)	**prohlídka** (f)	[progli:dka]

chase (pursuit)	stíhání (n)	[sti:ga:ni:]
to pursue, to chase	pronásledovat	[prona:slɛdovat]
to track (a criminal)	sledovat	[slɛdovat]

arrest	zatčení (n)	[zatʃeni:]
to arrest (sb)	zatknout	[zatknout]
to catch (thief, etc.)	chytit	[ɦɪtit]
capture	chycení (n)	[ɦɪtseni:]

document	dokument (m)	[dokumɛnt]
proof (evidence)	důkaz (m)	[du:kaz]
to prove (vt)	dokazovat	[dokazovat]
footprint	stopa (f)	[stopa]
fingerprints	otisky (m pl) prstů	[otiskɪ prstu:]
piece of evidence	důkaz (m)	[du:kaz]

alibi	alibi (n)	[alibi]
innocent (not guilty)	nevinný	[nɛwinɪ:]
injustice (unjust act)	nespravedlivost (f)	[nɛspravɛdlivost]
unjust, unfair (adj)	nespravedlivý	[nɛspra:vɛdlivɪ:]

crime (adj)	kriminální	[krimina:lni:]
to confiscate (vt)	konfiskovat	[konfiskovat]
drug (illegal substance)	droga (f)	[droga]
weapon, gun	zbraň (f)	[zbraɲ]
to disarm (vt)	odzbrojit	[odzbrojɪt]
to order (command)	rozkazovat	[rozkazovat]
to disappear (vi)	zmizet	[zmizɛt]

law	zákon (m)	[za:kon]
legal (adj)	zákonný	[za:konɪ:]
illegal (adj)	nezákonný	[nɛza:konɪ:]

| responsibility | odpovědnost (f) | [odpovʰednost] |
| responsible (adj) | odpovědný | [odpovʰednɪ:] |

NATURE

The Earth. Part 1

122. Outer space

cosmos	kosmos (m)	[kosmos]
space (as adj)	kosmický	[kosmitskɪ:]
outer space	kosmický prostor (m)	[kosmitskɪ: prostor]
universe	vesmír (m)	[vɛsmi:r]
galaxy	galaxie (f)	[galaksije]
star	hvězda (f)	[gvʰezda]
constellation	souhvězdí (n)	[sougvʰezdi:]
planet	planeta (f)	[planɛta]
satellite	družice (f)	[druʒiʦe]
meteorite	meteorit (m)	[mɛtɛorit]
comet	kometa (f)	[komɛta]
asteroid	asteroid (m)	[astɛroid]
orbit	oběžná dráha (f)	[obʰeʒna: dra:ga]
to rotate (vi)	otáčet se	[ota:ʧet sɛ]
atmosphere	atmosféra (f)	[atmosfɛ:ra]
the Sun	Slunce (n)	[slunʦɛ]
solar system	sluneční soustava (f)	[slunɛʧni: sɛstava]
solar eclipse	sluneční zatmění (n)	[slunɛʧni: zatmneni:]
the Earth	Země (f)	[zɛmne]
the Moon	Měsíc (m)	[mnesi:ʦ]
Mars	Mars (m)	[mars]
Venus	Venuše (f)	[vɛnuʃe]
Jupiter	Jupiter (m)	[jupitɛr]
Saturn	Saturn (m)	[saturn]
Mercury	Merkur (m)	[mɛrkur]
Uranus	Uran (m)	[uran]
Neptune	Neptun (m)	[nɛptun]
Pluto	Pluto (n)	[pluto]
Milky Way	Mléčná dráha (f)	[mlɛ:ʧna: dra:ga]
Great Bear	Velká medvědice (f)	[vɛlka: mɛdvʰediʦe]
North Star	Polárka (f)	[pola:rka]
Martian	Marťan (m)	[martʲan]
extraterrestrial	mimozemšťan (m)	[mimozɛmʃtʲan]

alien	vetřelec (m)	[vɛtrʃɛlɛts]
flying saucer	létající talíř (m)	[lɛ:tajɪ:tsi: tali:rʒ]
spaceship	kosmická loď (f)	[kosmitska: lodʲ]
space station	orbitální stanice (f)	[orbita:lni: stanitse]
blast-off	start (m)	[start]

engine	motor (m)	[motor]
nozzle	tryska (f)	[trɪska]
fuel	palivo (n)	[palivo]

cockpit, flight deck	kabina (f)	[kabina]
aerial	anténa (f)	[antɛ:na]
porthole	okénko (n)	[okɛ:ŋko]
solar battery	sluneční baterie (f)	[slunɛtʃni: batɛrie]
spacesuit	skafandr (m)	[skafandr]

| weightlessness | beztížný stav (m) | [bɛzti:ʒnɪ: stav] |
| oxygen | kyslík (m) | [kɪsli:k] |

| docking (in space) | spojení (n) | [spojeni:] |
| to dock (vi, vt) | spojovat se | [spojovat sɛ] |

| observatory | observatoř (f) | [obsɛrvatorʒ] |
| telescope | teleskop (m) | [tɛlɛskop] |

| to observe (vt) | pozorovat | [pozorovat] |
| to explore (vt) | zkoumat | [skoumat] |

123. The Earth

the Earth	Země (f)	[zɛmne]
globe (the Earth)	zeměkoule (f)	[zɛmnekoulɛ]
planet	planeta (f)	[planɛta]

atmosphere	atmosféra (f)	[atmosfɛ:ra]
geography	zeměpis (m)	[zɛmnepis]
nature	příroda (f)	[prʃi:roda]

globe (table ~)	glóbus (m)	[glo:bus]
map	mapa (f)	[mapa]
atlas	atlas (m)	[atlas]

| Europe | Evropa (f) | [ɛvropa] |
| Asia | Asie (f) | [azije] |

| Africa | Afrika (f) | [afrika] |
| Australia | Austrálie (f) | [austra:lije] |

America	Amerika (f)	[amɛrika]
North America	Severní Amerika (f)	[sɛvɛrni: amɛrika]
South America	Jižní Amerika (f)	[jɪʒni: amɛrika]

| Antarctica | Antarktida (f) | [antarktɪ:da] |
| the Arctic | Arktida (f) | [arktɪda] |

124. Cardinal directions

north	sever (m)	[sɛvɛr]
to the north	na sever	[na sɛvɛr]
in the north	na severu	[na sɛvɛru]
northern (adj)	severní	[sɛvɛrni:]
south	jih (m)	[jɪɦ]
to the south	na jih	[na jɪɦ]
in the south	na jihu	[na jɪgu]
southern (adj)	jižní	[jɪʒni:]
west	západ (m)	[za:pad]
to the west	na západ	[na za:pad]
in the west	na západě	[na za:pade]
western (adj)	západní	[za:padni:]
east	východ (m)	[vɪ:ɦod]
to the east	na východ	[na vɪ:ɦod]
in the east	na východě	[na vɪ:ɦode]
eastern (adj)	východní	[vɪ:ɦodni:]

125. Sea. Ocean

sea	moře (n)	[morʒe]
ocean	oceán (m)	[otsea:n]
gulf (bay)	záliv (m)	[za:liv]
straits	průliv (m)	[pru:liv]
continent (mainland)	pevnina (f)	[pɛvnina]
island	ostrov (m)	[ostrov]
peninsula	poloostrov (m)	[polo:strov]
archipelago	souostroví (n)	[souostrowi:]
bay	zátoka (f)	[za:toka]
harbour	přístav (m)	[prʃi:stav]
lagoon	laguna (f)	[lagu:na]
cape	mys (m)	[mɪs]
atoll	atol (m)	[atol]
reef	útes (m)	[u:tɛs]
coral	korál (m)	[kora:l]
coral reef	korálový útes (m)	[kora:lovɪ u:tɛs]
deep (adj)	hluboký	[glubokɪ:]
depth (deep water)	hloubka (f)	[gloubka]
abyss	hlubina (f)	[glubina]
trench (e.g. Mariana ~)	prohlubeň (f)	[proglubɛɲ]
current, stream	proud (m)	[prout]
to surround (bathe)	omývat	[omɪ:vat]
shore	břeh (m)	[brʒeɦ]
coast	pobřeží (n)	[pobrʒeʒi:]

high tide	příliv (m)	[prʃiːliv]
low tide	odliv (m)	[odliv]
sandbank	mělčina (f)	[mneltʃina]
bottom	dno (n)	[dno]

wave	vlna (f)	[vlna]
crest (~ of a wave)	hřbet (m) vlny	[grʒbɛt vlnɪ]
froth (foam)	pěna (f)	[pʰena]

hurricane	hurikán (m)	[gurikaːn]
tsunami	tsunami (n)	[tsunami]
calm (dead ~)	bezvětří (n)	[bɛzvʰetrʃiː]
quiet, calm (adj)	klidný	[klidnɪː]

| pole | pól (m) | [poːl] |
| polar (adj) | polární | [polaːrniː] |

latitude	šířka (f)	[ʃiːrʃka]
longitude	délka (f)	[dɛːlka]
parallel	rovnoběžka (f)	[rovnobʰeʒka]
equator	rovník (m)	[rovniːk]

sky	obloha (f)	[obloga]
horizon	horizont (m)	[gorizont]
air	vzduch (m)	[vzduɦ]

lighthouse	maják (m)	[majaːk]
to dive (vi)	potápět se	[potaːpʰet sɛ]
to sink (ab. boat)	potopit se	[potopit sɛ]
treasures	bohatství (n)	[bogatstwiː]

126. Seas & Oceans names

Atlantic Ocean	Atlantický oceán (m)	[atlantɪtskɪ: otsea:n]
Indian Ocean	Indický oceán (m)	[indɪtskɪ: otsea:n]
Pacific Ocean	Tichý oceán (m)	[tiɦɪ: otsea:n]
Arctic Ocean	Severní ledový oceán (m)	[sɛvɛrni: lɛdovɪ: otsea:n]

Black Sea	Černé moře (n)	[tʃernɛ: morʒe]
Red Sea	Rudé moře (n)	[rudɛ: morʒe]
Yellow Sea	Žluté moře (n)	[ʒlutɛ: morʒɛ]
White Sea	Bílé moře (n)	[biːlɛ: morʒɛ]

Caspian Sea	Kaspické moře (n)	[kaspitskɛ: morʒe]
Dead Sea	Mrtvé moře (n)	[mrtvɛ: morʒe]
Mediterranean Sea	Středozemní moře (n)	[strʃedozɛmni: morʒe]

| Aegean Sea | Egejské moře (n) | [ɛgɛjskɛ: morʒe] |
| Adriatic Sea | Jaderské moře (n) | [jadɛrskɛ: morʒe] |

Arabian Sea	Arabské moře (n)	[arabskɛ: morʒɛ]
Sea of Japan	Japonské moře (n)	[japonskɛ: morʒɛ]
Bering Sea	Beringovo moře (n)	[bɛriŋovo morʒɛ]
South China Sea	Jihočínské moře (n)	[jɪgotʃi:nskɛ: morʒɛ]

Coral Sea	Korálové moře (n)	[kora:lovɛ: morʒɛ]
Tasman Sea	Tasmanovo moře (n)	[tasmanovo morʒɛ]
Caribbean Sea	Karibské moře (n)	[karibskɛ: morʒe]
Barents Sea	Barentsovo moře (n)	[barɛntsovo morʒɛ]
Kara Sea	Karské moře (n)	[karskɛ: morʒɛ]
North Sea	Severní moře (n)	[sɛvɛrni: morʒe]
Baltic Sea	Baltské moře (n)	[baltskɛ: morʒe]
Norwegian Sea	Norské moře (n)	[norskɛ: morʒɛ]

127. Mountains

mountain	hora (f)	[gora]
mountain range	horské pásmo (n)	[gorskɛ: pa:smo]
mountain ridge	horský hřbet (m)	[gorskɪ: grʒbɛt]
summit, top	vrchol (m)	[vrɦol]
peak	štít (m)	[ʃti:t]
foot (of mountain)	úpatí (n)	[u:pati:]
slope (mountainside)	svah (m)	[svaɦ]
volcano	sopka (f)	[sopka]
active volcano	činná sopka (f)	[tʃina: sopka]
dormant volcano	vyhaslá sopka (f)	[vɪgasla: sopka]
eruption	výbuch (m)	[vɪ:buɦ]
crater	kráter (m)	[kra:tɛr]
magma	magma (f)	[magma]
lava	láva (f)	[la:va]
molten (~ lava)	rozžhavený	[rozʒgavɛnɪ:]
canyon	kaňon (m)	[kanɜn]
gorge	soutěska (f)	[soutɛska]
crevice	rozsedlina (f)	[rozsɛdlina]
pass, col	průsmyk (m)	[pru:smɪk]
plateau	plató (n)	[plato:]
cliff	skála (f)	[ska:la]
hill	kopec (m)	[kopɛts]
glacier	ledovec (m)	[lɛdovɛts]
waterfall	vodopád (m)	[vodopa:d]
geyser	vřídlo (n)	[vrʒi:dlo]
lake	jezero (n)	[jezɛro]
plain	rovina (f)	[rowina]
landscape	krajina (f)	[krajɪna]
echo	ozvěna (f)	[ozvʰena]
alpinist	horolezec (m)	[gorolɛzɛts]
rock climber	horolezec (m)	[gorolɛzɛts]
to conquer (in climbing)	dobývat	[dobɪ:vat]
climb (an easy ~)	výstup (m)	[vɪ:stup]

128. Mountains names

Alps	Alpy (pl)	[alpɪ]
Mont Blanc	Mont blank (m)	[montblaŋk]
Pyrenees	Pyreneje (pl)	[pɪrɛnɛje]
Carpathians	Karpaty (pl)	[karpatɪ]
Ural Mountains	Ural (m)	[ural]
Caucasus	Kavkaz (m)	[kavkaz]
Elbrus	Elbrus (m)	[ɛʎbrus]
Altai	Altaj (m)	[altaj]
Tien Shan	Ťan-šan (f)	[tʲan ʃan]
Pamir Mountains	Pamír (m)	[pami:r]
Himalayas	Himaláje (pl)	[gimala:jɛ]
Everest	Mount Everest (m)	[mount ɛvɛrɛst]
Andes	Andy (pl)	[andɪ]
Kilimanjaro	Kilimandžáro (n)	[kilimanʤa:ro]

129. Rivers

river	řeka (f)	[rʒeka]
spring (natural source)	pramen (m)	[pramɛn]
riverbed	koryto (n)	[korɪto]
basin	povodí (n)	[povodi:]
to flow into …	vlévat se	[vlɛ:vat sɛ]
tributary	přítok (m)	[prʃi:tok]
bank (of river)	břeh (m)	[brʒeɦ]
current, stream	proud (m)	[prout]
downstream (adv)	po proudu	[po proudu]
upstream (adv)	proti proudu	[proti proudu]
flood	povodeň (f)	[povodɛɲ]
flooding	záplava (f)	[za:plava]
to overflow (vi)	rozlévat se	[rozlɛ:vat sɛ]
to flood (vt)	zaplavovat	[zaplavovat]
shallows (shoal)	mělčina (f)	[mneltʃina]
rapids	peřej (f)	[pɛrʒej]
dam	přehrada (f)	[prʃɛgrada]
canal	průplav (m)	[pru:plav]
reservoir (artificial lake)	vodní nádrž (f)	[vodni: na:drʒ]
sluice, lock	zdymadlo (n)	[zdɪmadlo]
water body (pond, etc.)	vodojem (m)	[vodojem]
swamp, bog	bažina (f)	[baʒina]
marsh	bažina (f)	[baʒina]
whirlpool	vír (m)	[wi:r]
stream (brook)	potok (m)	[potok]

| drinking (ab. water) | pitný | [pitnɪ:] |
| fresh (~ water) | sladký | [sladkɪ:] |

| ice | led (m) | [lɛd] |
| to ice over | zamrznout | [zamrznout] |

130. Rivers names

| Seine | Seina (f) | [se:na] |
| Loire | Loira (f) | [loa:ra] |

Thames	Temže (f)	[tɛmʒɛ]
Rhine	Rýn (m)	[rɪ:n]
Danube	Dunaj (m)	[dunaj]

Volga	Volha (f)	[volga]
Don	Don (m)	[don]
Lena	Lena (f)	[lɛna]

Yellow River	Chuang-chež (f)	[ɦuanɦɛ]
Yangtze	Jang-c'-t'iang (f)	[jaɲtsɛtʹaŋ]
Mekong	Mekong (m)	[mɛkoŋ]
Ganges	Ganga (f)	[gaŋa]

Nile	Nil (m)	[nɪl]
Congo	Kongo (n)	[koŋo]
Okavango	Okavango (n)	[okavaŋo]
Zambezi	Zambezi (f)	[zambɛzi]
Limpopo	Limpopo (n)	[lɪmpopo]
Mississippi River	Mississippi (f)	[misisipi]

131. Forest

| forest | les (m) | [lɛs] |
| forest (as adj) | lesní | [lɛsni:] |

thick forest	houština (f)	[gouʃtina]
grove	háj (m)	[ga:j]
clearing	mýtina (f)	[mɪ:tina]

| thicket | houští (n) | [gouʃti:] |
| scrubland | křoví (n) | [krʃowi:] |

| footpath | stezka (f) | [stɛzka] |
| gully | rokle (f) | [roklɛ] |

tree	strom (m)	[strom]
leaf	list (m)	[list]
leaves	listí (n)	[listi:]

| falling leaves | padání (n) listí | [pada:ni: listi:] |
| to fall (ab. leaves) | opadávat | [opada:vat] |

top (of the tree)	vrchol (m)	[vrɦol]
branch	větev (f)	[vʰetɛv]
bough	suk (m)	[suk]
bud (on shrub, tree)	pupen (m)	[pupɛn]
needle (of pine tree)	jehla (f)	[jegla]
fir cone	šiška (f)	[ʃiʃka]

hollow (in a tree)	dutina (f)	[dutina]
nest	hnízdo (n)	[gniːzdo]
burrow (animal hole)	doupě (n)	[doupʰe]

trunk	kmen (m)	[kmɛn]
root	kořen (m)	[korʒen]
bark	kůra (f)	[kuːra]
moss	mech (m)	[mɛɦ]

to uproot (vt)	klučit	[klutʃit]
to chop down	kácet	[kaːtset]
to deforest (vt)	odlesnit	[odlesnit]
tree stump	pařez (m)	[parʒez]

campfire	oheň (m)	[ogɛɲ]
forest fire	požár (m)	[poʒaːr]
to extinguish (vt)	hasit	[gasit]

forest ranger	hajný (m)	[gajnɪː]
protection	ochrana (f)	[oɦrana]
to protect (~ nature)	chránit	[ɦraːnit]
poacher	pytlák (m)	[pɪtlaːk]
trap (e.g. bear ~)	past (f)	[past]

to gather, to pick (vt)	sbírat	[sbiːrat]
to lose one's way	zabloudit	[zabloudit]

132. Natural resources

natural resources	přírodní zdroje (m pl)	[prʃiːrodni zdroje]
minerals	užitkové nerosty (m pl)	[uʒitkovɛː nɛrostɪ]
deposits	ložisko (n)	[loʒisko]
field (e.g. oilfield)	ložisko (n)	[loʒisko]

to mine (extract)	dobývat	[dobɪːvat]
mining (extraction)	těžba (f)	[teʒba]
ore	ruda (f)	[ruda]
mine (e.g. for coal)	důl (m)	[duːl]
mine shaft, pit	šachta (f)	[ʃaɦta]
miner	horník (m)	[gorniːk]

gas	plyn (m)	[plɪn]
gas pipeline	plynovod (m)	[plɪnovod]

oil (petroleum)	ropa (f)	[ropa]
oil pipeline	ropovod (m)	[ropovod]
oil rig	ropová věž (f)	[ropovaː vʰeʒ]

| derrick | vrtná věž (f) | [vrtna: vʰeʒ] |
| tanker | tanková loď (f) | [taŋkova: lodʲ] |

sand	písek (m)	[pi:sɛk]
limestone	vápenec (m)	[va:pɛnɛts]
gravel	štěrk (m)	[ʃterk]
peat	rašelina (f)	[raʃɛlina]
clay	hlína (f)	[gli:na]
coal	uhlí (n)	[ugli:]

iron	železo (n)	[ʒelɛzo]
gold	zlato (n)	[zlato]
silver	stříbro (n)	[strʃi:bro]
nickel	nikl (m)	[nɪkl]
copper	měď (f)	[mnedʲ]

zinc	zinek (m)	[zinɛk]
manganese	mangan (m)	[maŋan]
mercury	rtuť (f)	[rtutʲ]
lead	olovo (n)	[olovo]

mineral	minerál (m)	[minɛra:l]
crystal	krystal (m)	[kristal]
marble	mramor (m)	[mramor]
uranium	uran (m)	[uran]

The Earth. Part 2

133. Weather

weather	počasí (n)	[potʃasi:]
weather forecast	předpověď (f) počasí	[prʃɛdpovʰedʲ potʃasi:]
temperature	teplota (f)	[tɛplota]
thermometer	teploměr (m)	[tɛplomner]
barometer	barometr (m)	[baromɛtr]
humidity	vlhkost (f)	[vlɦkost]
heat (of summer)	horko (n)	[gorko]
hot (torrid)	horký	[gorkɪ:]
it's hot	horko	[gorko]
it's warm	teplo	[tɛplo]
warm (moderately hot)	teplý	[tɛplɪ:]
it's cold	je zima	[je zima]
cold (adj)	studený	[studɛnɪ:]
sun	slunce (n)	[sluntsɛ]
to shine (vi)	svítit	[swi:tit]
sunny (day)	slunečný	[slunɛtʃnɪ:]
to come up (vi)	vzejít	[vzɛjɪ:t]
to set (vi)	zapadnout	[zapadnout]
cloud	mrak (m)	[mrak]
cloudy (adj)	oblačný	[oblatʃnɪ:]
rain cloud	mračno (n)	[mratʃno]
somber (gloomy)	pochmurný	[poɦmurnɪ:]
rain	déšť (m)	[dɛ:ʃtʲ]
it's raining	prší	[prʃi:]
rainy (day)	deštivý	[dɛʃtivɪ:]
to drizzle (vi)	mrholit	[mrɡolit]
pouring rain	liják (m)	[lija:k]
downpour	liják (m)	[lija:k]
heavy (e.g. ~ rain)	silný	[silnɪ:]
puddle	kaluž (f)	[kaluʒ]
to get wet (in rain)	moknout	[moknout]
mist (fog)	mlha (f)	[mlɡa]
misty (adj)	mlhavý	[mlɡavɪ:]
snow	sníh (m)	[sni:ɦ]
it's snowing	sněží	[snɛʒi:]

134. Severe weather. Natural disasters

thunderstorm	bouřka (f)	[bourʒka]
lightning (~ strike)	blesk (m)	[blɛsk]
to flash (vi)	blýskat se	[blɪːskat sɛ]
thunder	hřmění (n)	[grʒmneniː]
to thunder (vi)	hřmít	[grʒmiːt]
it's thundering	hřmí	[grʒmiː]
hail	kroupy (f pl)	[kroupɪ]
it's hailing	padají kroupy	[padajɪ: kroupɪ]
to flood (vt)	zaplavit	[zaplawit]
flood	povodeň (f)	[povodɛɲ]
earthquake	zemětřesení (n)	[zɛmnetrʃɛsɛniː]
tremor, quake	otřes (m)	[otrʃɛs]
epicentre	epicentrum (n)	[ɛpiʦentrum]
eruption	výbuch (m)	[vɪːbuɦ]
lava	láva (f)	[laːva]
twister	smršť (f)	[smrʃtʲ]
tornado	tornádo (n)	[tornaːdo]
typhoon	tajfun (m)	[tajfun]
hurricane	hurikán (m)	[gurikaːn]
storm	bouřka (f)	[bourʒka]
tsunami	tsunami (n)	[ʦunami]
cyclone	cyklón (m)	[ʦikloːn]
bad weather	nečas (m)	[nɛʧas]
fire (accident)	požár (m)	[poʒaːr]
disaster	katastrofa (f)	[katastrofa]
meteorite	meteorit (m)	[mɛtɛorit]
avalanche	lavina (f)	[lawina]
snowslide	lavina (f)	[lawina]
blizzard	metelice (f)	[mɛtɛliʦe]
snowstorm	vánice (f)	[vaːniʦe]

Fauna

135. Mammals. Predators

predator	šelma (f)	[ʃɛlma]
tiger	tygr (m)	[tɪgr]
lion	lev (m)	[lɛv]
wolf	vlk (m)	[vlk]
fox	liška (f)	[liʃka]

jaguar	jaguár (m)	[jaguaːr]
leopard	levhart (m)	[lɛvgart]
cheetah	gepard (m)	[gɛpard]

black panther	panter (m)	[pantɛr]
puma	puma (f)	[puma]
snow leopard	pardál (m)	[pardaːl]
lynx	rys (m)	[rɪs]

coyote	kojot (m)	[kojot]
jackal	šakal (m)	[ʃakal]
hyena	hyena (f)	[gijena]

136. Wild animals

animal	zvíře (n)	[zwiːrʒe]
beast (animal)	zvíře (n)	[zwiːrʒe]

squirrel	veverka (f)	[vɛvɛrka]
hedgehog	ježek (m)	[jeʒek]
hare	zajíc (m)	[zajɪːts]
rabbit	králík (m)	[kraːliːk]

badger	jezevec (m)	[jɛzɛvɛts]
raccoon	mýval (m)	[mɪːval]
hamster	křeček (m)	[krʃɛtʃek]
marmot	svišť (m)	[swiʃtʲ]

mole	krtek (m)	[krtɛk]
mouse	myš (f)	[mɪʃ]
rat	krysa (f)	[krɪsa]
bat	netopýr (m)	[nɛtopɪːr]

ermine	hranostaj (m)	[granostaj]
sable	sobol (m)	[sobol]
marten	kuna (f)	[kuna]
weasel	lasice (f)	[lasitse]
mink	norek (m)	[norɛk]

| beaver | bobr (m) | [bobr] |
| otter | vydra (f) | [vɪdra] |

horse	kůň (m)	[ku:ɲ]
moose	los (m)	[los]
deer	jelen (m)	[jelɛn]
camel	velbloud (m)	[vɛlbloud]

bison	bizon (m)	[bizon]
aurochs	zubr (m)	[zubr]
buffalo	buvol (m)	[buvol]

zebra	zebra (f)	[zɛbra]
antelope	antilopa (f)	[antɪlopa]
roe deer	srnka (f)	[srɲka]
fallow deer	daněk (m)	[danek]
chamois	kamzík (m)	[kamzi:k]
wild boar	vepř (m)	[vɛprʃ]

whale	velryba (f)	[vɛlrɪba]
seal	tuleň (m)	[tulɛɲ]
walrus	mrož (m)	[mroʒ]
fur seal	lachtan (m)	[laɦtan]
dolphin	delfín (m)	[dɛlfi:n]

bear	medvěd (m)	[mɛdvʰed]
polar bear	bílý medvěd (m)	[bi:lɪ: mɛdvʰed]
panda	panda (f)	[panda]

monkey	opice (f)	[opiʦe]
chimpanzee	šimpanz (m)	[ʃimpanz]
orangutan	orangutan (m)	[oraɲutan]
gorilla	gorila (f)	[gorila]
macaque	makak (m)	[makak]
gibbon	gibon (m)	[gibon]

elephant	slon (m)	[slon]
rhinoceros	nosorožec (m)	[nosoroʒeʦ]
giraffe	žirafa (f)	[ʒirafa]
hippopotamus	hroch (m)	[groɦ]

| kangaroo | klokan (m) | [klokan] |
| koala (bear) | koala (f) | [koala] |

mongoose	promyka (f) indická	[promɪka indɪtska:]
chinchilla	činčila (f)	[tʃintʃila]
skunk	skunk (m)	[skuɲk]
porcupine	dikobraz (m)	[dikobraz]

137. Domestic animals

cat	kočka (f)	[kotʃka]
tomcat	kocour (m)	[kotsour]
dog	pes (m)	[pɛs]

horse	kůň (m)	[ku:ɲ]
stallion	hřebec (m)	[grʒebɛts]
mare	kobyla (f)	[kobɪla]

cow	kráva (f)	[kra:va]
bull	býk (m)	[bɪ:k]
ox	vůl (m)	[vu:l]

sheep	ovce (f)	[ovtse]
ram	beran (m)	[bɛran]
goat	koza (f)	[koza]
billy goat, he-goat	kozel (m)	[kozɛl]

| donkey | osel (m) | [osɛl] |
| mule | mul (m) | [mul] |

pig	prase (n)	[prasɛ]
piglet	prasátko (n)	[prasa:tko]
rabbit	králík (m)	[kra:li:k]

| hen (chicken) | slepice (f) | [slɛpitse] |
| cock | kohout (m) | [kogout] |

duck	kachna (f)	[kaɦna]
drake	kačer (m)	[katʃer]
goose	husa (f)	[gusa]

| stag turkey | krocan (m) | [krotsan] |
| turkey (hen) | krůta (f) | [kru:ta] |

domestic animals	domácí zvířata (n pl)	[doma:tsi: zwi:rʒata]
tame (e.g. ~ hamster)	ochočený	[oɦotʃenɪ:]
to tame (vt)	ochočovat	[oɦotʃovat]
to breed (vt)	chovat	[ɦovat]

farm	farma (f)	[farma]
poultry	drůbež (f)	[dru:bɛʒ]
cattle	dobytek (m)	[dobɪtɛk]
herd (cattle)	stádo (n)	[sta:do]

stable	stáj (f)	[sta:j]
pigsty	vepřín (m)	[vɛprʃi:n]
cowshed	kravín (m)	[krawi:n]
rabbit hutch	králíkárna (f)	[kra:li:ka:rna]
hen house	kurník (m)	[kurni:k]

138. Birds

bird	pták (m)	[pta:k]
pigeon	holub (m)	[golub]
sparrow	vrabec (m)	[vrabɛts]
tit	sýkora (f)	[sɪ:kora]
magpie	straka (f)	[straka]
raven	havran (m)	[gavran]

crow	vrána (f)	[vraːna]
jackdaw	kavka (f)	[kavka]
rook	polní havran (m)	[polniː gavran]

duck	kachna (f)	[kaɦna]
goose	husa (f)	[gusa]
pheasant	bažant (m)	[baʒant]

eagle	orel (m)	[orɛl]
hawk	jestřáb (m)	[jestrʃaːb]
falcon	sokol (m)	[sokol]
vulture	sup (m)	[sup]
condor	kondor (m)	[kondor]

swan	labuť (f)	[labutʲ]
crane	jeřáb (m)	[jerʒaːb]
stork	čáp (m)	[ʧaːp]

parrot	papoušek (m)	[papouʃɛk]
hummingbird	kolibřík (m)	[kolibrʒiːk]
peacock	páv (m)	[paːv]

ostrich	pštros (m)	[pʃtros]
heron	volavka (f)	[volavka]
flamingo	plameňák (m)	[plamɛɲaːk]
pelican	pelikán (m)	[pɛlikaːn]

| nightingale | slavík (m) | [slawiːk] |
| swallow | vlaštovka (f) | [vlaʃtovka] |

thrush	drozd (m)	[drozd]
song thrush	zpěvný drozd (m)	[spʰevnɪː drozd]
blackbird	kos (m)	[kos]

swift	rorejs (m)	[rorɛjs]
lark	skřivan (m)	[skrʃivan]
quail	křepel (m)	[krʃɛpɛl]

woodpecker	datel (m)	[datɛl]
cuckoo	kukačka (f)	[kukaʧka]
owl	sova (f)	[sova]
eagle owl	výr (m)	[vɪːr]
wood grouse	tetřev (m) hlušec	[tɛtrʃɛv gluʃɛts]
black grouse	tetřev (m)	[tɛtrʃɛv]
partridge	koroptev (f)	[koroptɛv]

starling	špaček (m)	[ʃpaʧek]
canary	kanár (m)	[kanaːr]
hazel grouse	jeřábek (m)	[jerʒaːbɛk]

| chaffinch | pěnkava (f) | [pʰeŋkava] |
| bullfinch | hejl (m) | [gɛjl] |

seagull	racek (m)	[ratsek]
albatross	albatros (m)	[albatros]
penguin	tučňák (m)	[tuʧɲaːk]

139. Fish. Marine animals

bream	cejn (m)	[ʦejn]
carp	kapr (m)	[kapr]
perch	okoun (m)	[okoun]
catfish	sumec (m)	[sumɛʦ]
pike	štika (f)	[ʃtika]

| salmon | losos (m) | [losos] |
| sturgeon | jeseter (m) | [jesɛtɛr] |

herring	sleď (f)	[slɛdʲ]
Atlantic salmon	losos (m)	[losos]
mackerel	makrela (f)	[makrɛla]
flatfish	platýs (m)	[platɪːs]

zander, pike perch	candát (m)	[ʦandaːt]
cod	treska (f)	[trɛska]
tuna	tuňák (m)	[tuɲaːk]
trout	pstruh (m)	[pstruɦ]

eel	úhoř (m)	[uːgorʒ]
electric ray	rejnok (m) elektrický	[rɛjnok ɛlɛktriʦkɪː]
moray eel	muréna (f)	[murɛːna]
piranha	piraňa (f)	[piraɲa]

shark	žralok (m)	[ʒralok]
dolphin	delfín (m)	[dɛlfiːn]
whale	velryba (f)	[vɛlrɪba]

crab	krab (m)	[krab]
jellyfish	medúza (f)	[mɛduːza]
octopus	chobotnice (f)	[ɦobotniʦe]

starfish	hvězdice (f)	[gvʰezdiʦe]
sea urchin	ježovka (f)	[jeʒovka]
seahorse	mořský koníček (m)	[morʃskɪː koniːʧek]

oyster	ústřice (f)	[uːstrʃiʦe]
prawn	kreveta (f)	[krɛvɛta]
lobster	humr (m)	[gumr]
spiny lobster	langusta (f)	[laŋusta]

140. Amphibians. Reptiles

| snake | had (m) | [gad] |
| venomous (snake) | jedovatý | [jedovatɪː] |

viper	zmije (f)	[zmije]
cobra	kobra (f)	[kobra]
python	krajta (f)	[krajta]
boa	hroznýš (m)	[groznɪːʃ]
grass snake	užovka (f)	[uʒovka]

| rattle snake | chřestýš (m) | [ĥrʃɛstɪːʃ] |
| anaconda | anakonda (f) | [anakonda] |

lizard	ještěrka (f)	[jeʃterka]
iguana	leguán (m)	[lɛguaːn]
monitor lizard	varan (m)	[varan]
salamander	mlok (m)	[mlok]
chameleon	chameleón (m)	[ĥamɛlɛoːn]
scorpion	štír (m)	[ʃtiːr]

turtle	želva (f)	[ʒelva]
frog	žába (f)	[ʒaːba]
toad	ropucha (f)	[ropuĥa]
crocodile	krokodýl (m)	[krokodɪːl]

141. Insects

insect	hmyz (m)	[gmɪz]
butterfly	motýl (m)	[motɪːl]
ant	mravenec (m)	[mravɛnɛts]
fly	moucha (f)	[mouĥa]
mosquito	komár (m)	[komaːr]
beetle	brouk (m)	[brouk]

wasp	vosa (f)	[vosa]
bee	včela (f)	[vtʃela]
bumblebee	čmelák (m)	[tʃmɛlaːk]
gadfly	střeček (m)	[strʃɛtʃek]

| spider | pavouk (m) | [pavouk] |
| spider's web | pavučina (f) | [pavutʃina] |

dragonfly	vážka (f)	[vaːʒka]
grasshopper	kobylka (f)	[kobɪlka]
moth (night butterfly)	motýl (m)	[motɪːl]

cockroach	šváb (m)	[ʃvaːb]
tick	klíště (n)	[kliːʃte]
flea	blecha (f)	[blɛĥa]
midge	muška (f)	[muʃka]

locust	saranče (f)	[sarantʃe]
snail	hlemýžď (m)	[glɛmɪːʒdʲ]
cricket	cvrček (m)	[tsvrtʃek]
firefly	svatojánská muška (f)	[svatojaːnska: muʃka]
ladybird	slunéčko (n) sedmitečné	[slunɛːtʃko sɛdmitɛtʃnɛː]
cockchafer	chroust (m)	[ĥroust]

leech	pijavice (f)	[pijawitse]
caterpillar	housenka (f)	[gousɛŋka]
earthworm	červ (m)	[tʃerv]
larva	larva (f)	[larva]

Flora

142. Trees

tree	strom (m)	[strom]
deciduous (adj)	listnatý	[listnatɪ:]
coniferous (adj)	jehličnatý	[eglitʃnatɪ:]
evergreen (adj)	stálezelená	[sta:lɛzɛlɛna:]
apple tree	jabloň (f)	[jabloɲ]
pear tree	hruška (f)	[gruʃka]
sweet cherry tree	třešně (f)	[trʃɛʃne]
sour cherry tree	višně (f)	[wiʃne]
plum tree	švestka (f)	[ʃvɛstka]
birch	bříza (f)	[brʒi:za]
oak	dub (m)	[dub]
linden tree	lípa (f)	[li:pa]
aspen	osika (f)	[osika]
maple	javor (m)	[javor]
spruce	smrk (m)	[smrk]
pine	borovice (f)	[borowitse]
larch	modřín (m)	[modrʒi:n]
fir	jedle (f)	[jedlɛ]
cedar	cedr (m)	[tsedr]
poplar	topol (m)	[topol]
rowan	jeřáb (m)	[jerʒa:b]
willow	jíva (f)	[jɪ:va]
alder	olše (f)	[olʃɛ]
beech	buk (m)	[buk]
elm	jilm (m)	[jɪlm]
ash (tree)	jasan (m)	[jasan]
chestnut	kaštan (m)	[kaʃtan]
magnolia	magnólie (f)	[magno:lije]
palm tree	palma (f)	[palma]
cypress	cypřiš (m)	[tsiprʃiʃ]
mangrove	mangróvie (f)	[maɲro:wiɛ]
baobab	baobab (m)	[baobab]
eucalyptus	eukalypt (m)	[ɛukalipt]
sequoia	sekvoje (f)	[sɛkvoje]

143. Shrubs

bush	keř (m)	[kɛrʒ]
shrub	křoví (n)	[krʃowi:]

| grapevine | vinná réva (n) | [wiɲa: reːva] |
| vineyard | vinice (f) | [winitse] |

raspberry bush	maliny (f pl)	[malɪnɪ]
redcurrant bush	červený rybíz (m)	[t͡ʃɛrvɛnɪ rɪbiːz]
gooseberry bush	angrešt (m)	[aŋrɛʃt]

acacia	akácie (f)	[akaːt͡sije]
barberry	dřišťál (m)	[drʒɪʃtʼaːl]
jasmine	jasmín (m)	[jasmiːn]

juniper	jalovec (m)	[jalovɛt͡s]
rosebush	růžový keř (m)	[ruːʒovɪ kɛrʒ]
dog rose	šípek (m)	[ʃiːpɛk]

144. Fruits. Berries

apple	jablko (n)	[jablko]
pear	hruška (f)	[gruʃka]
plum	švestka (f)	[ʃvɛstka]
strawberry	zahradní jahody (f pl)	[zagradni: jagodɪ]
sour cherry	višně (f)	[wiʃɲe]
sweet cherry	třešně (f pl)	[trʃɛʃne]
grape	hroznové víno (n)	[groznovɛ: wiːno]

raspberry	maliny (f pl)	[malɪnɪ]
blackcurrant	černý rybíz (m)	[t͡ʃɛrnɪ rɪbiːz]
redcurrant	červený rybíz (m)	[t͡ʃɛrvɛnɪ rɪbiːz]
gooseberry	angrešt (m)	[aŋrɛʃt]
cranberry	klikva (f)	[klikva]

orange	pomeranč (m)	[pomɛrant͡ʃ]
tangerine	mandarinka (f)	[mandarɪŋka]
pineapple	ananas (m)	[ananas]
banana	banán (m)	[banaːn]
date	datle (f)	[datlɛ]
lemon	citrón (m)	[t͡sitroːn]
apricot	meruňka (f)	[mɛruɲka]
peach	broskev (f)	[broskɛv]
kiwi	kiwi (n)	[kiwi]
grapefruit	grapefruit (m)	[grɛjpfruːt]

berry	bobule (f)	[bobulɛ]
berries	bobule (f pl)	[bobulɛ]
cowberry	brusinky (f pl)	[brusɪŋkɪ]
wild strawberry	jahody (f pl)	[jagodɪ]
bilberry	borůvky (f pl)	[boruːvkɪ]

145. Flowers. Plants

| flower | květina (f) | [kvʰetina] |
| bouquet (of flowers) | kytice (f) | [kɪtit͡se] |

rose (flower)	růže (f)	[ru:ʒe]
tulip	tulipán (m)	[tulipa:n]
carnation	karafiát (m)	[karafija:t]
gladiolus	mečík (m)	[mɛtʃi:k]

cornflower	chrpa (f)	[ɦrpa]
bluebell	zvoneček (m)	[zvonɛtʃek]
dandelion	pampeliška (f)	[pampɛliʃka]
camomile	heřmánek (m)	[gɛrʒma:nɛk]

aloe	aloe (n)	[aloɛ]
cactus	kaktus (m)	[kaktus]
rubber plant	fíkus (m)	[fi:kus]

lily	lilie (f)	[lilije]
geranium	geránie (f)	[gera:nije]
hyacinth	hyacint (m)	[gijaʦint]

mimosa	citlivka (f)	[ʦitlivka]
narcissus	narcis (m)	[narʦis]
nasturtium	potočnice (f)	[pototʃniʦe]

orchid	orchidej (f)	[orɦidɛj]
peony	pivoňka (f)	[pivoɲka]
violet	fialka (f)	[fijalka]

pansy	maceška (f)	[maʦeʃka]
forget-me-not	pomněnka (f)	[pomnɛɲka]
daisy	sedmikráska (f)	[sɛdmikra:ska]

poppy	mák (m)	[ma:k]
hemp	konopě (f)	[konopʰe]
mint	máta (f)	[ma:ta]

| lily of the valley | konvalinka (f) | [konvaliɲka] |
| snowdrop | sněženka (f) | [sneʒeɲka] |

nettle	kopřiva (f)	[koprʃiva]
sorrel	šťovík (m)	[ʃtʒwi:k]
water lily	leknín (m)	[lɛkni:n]
fern	kapradí (n)	[kapradi:]
lichen	lišejník (m)	[liʃɛjni:k]

tropical glasshouse	oranžérie (f)	[oranʒe:rije]
grass lawn	trávník (m)	[tra:vni:k]
flowerbed	květinový záhonek (m)	[kvʰetinovɪ za:gonɛk]

plant	rostlina (f)	[rostlina]
grass	tráva (f)	[tra:va]
blade of grass	stéblo (n) trávy	[stɛ:blo tra:vɪ]

leaf	list (m)	[list]
petal	okvětní lístek (m)	[okvʰetni: li:stɛk]
stem	stéblo (n)	[stɛ:blo]
tuber	hlíza (f)	[gli:za]
young plant (shoot)	výhonek (m)	[vɪ:gonɛk]

thorn	osten (m)	[ostɛn]
to blossom (vi)	kvést	[kvɛ:st]
to fade, to wither	vadnout	[vadnout]
smell (odour)	vůně (f)	[vu:ne]
to cut (flowers)	uříznout	[urʒi:znout]
to pick (a flower)	utrhnout	[utrgnout]

146. Cereals, grains

grain	obilí (n)	[obili:]
cereals (plants)	obilniny (f pl)	[obilninɪ]
ear (of barley, etc.)	klas (m)	[klas]
wheat	pšenice (f)	[pʃɛnitse]
rye	žito (n)	[ʒito]
oats	oves (m)	[ovɛs]
millet	jáhly (f pl)	[ja:glɪ]
barley	ječmen (m)	[jetʃmɛn]
maize	kukuřice (f)	[kukurʒitse]
rice	rýže (f)	[rɪ:ʒe]
buckwheat	pohanka (f)	[pogaŋka]
pea	hrách (m)	[gra:ɦ]
kidney bean	fazole (f)	[fazolɛ]
soya	sója (f)	[so:ja]
lentil	čočka (f)	[tʃotʃka]
beans (broad ~)	boby (m pl)	[bobɪ]

COUNTRIES. NATIONALITIES

147. Western Europe

Europe	Evropa (f)	[ɛvropa]
European Union	Evropská unie (f)	[ɛuropska: uniɛ]
Austria	Rakousko (n)	[rakousko]
Great Britain	Velká Británie (f)	[vɛlka: brɪta:niɛ]
England	Anglie (f)	[aŋlije]
Belgium	Belgie (f)	[bɛlgije]
Germany	Německo (n)	[nemɛtsko]
Netherlands	Nizozemí (n)	[nizozɛmi:]
Holland	Holandsko (n)	[golandsko]
Greece	Řecko (n)	[rʒetsko]
Denmark	Dánsko (n)	[da:nsko]
Ireland	Irsko (n)	[irsko]
Iceland	Island (m)	[island]
Spain	Španělsko (n)	[ʃpanelsko]
Italy	Itálie (f)	[ita:lije]
Cyprus	Kypr (m)	[kipr]
Malta	Malta (f)	[malta]
Norway	Norsko (n)	[norsko]
Portugal	Portugalsko (n)	[portugalsko]
Finland	Finsko (n)	[finsko]
France	Francie (f)	[frantsije]
Sweden	Švédsko (n)	[ʃvɛ:dsko]
Switzerland	Švýcarsko (n)	[ʃvɪ:tsarsko]
Scotland	Skotsko (n)	[skotsko]
Vatican	Vatikán (m)	[vatɪka:n]
Liechtenstein	Lichtenštejnsko (n)	[lɪhtɛnʃtɛjnsko]
Luxembourg	Lucembursko (n)	[lutsembursko]
Monaco	Monako (n)	[monako]

148. Central and Eastern Europe

Albania	Albánie (f)	[alba:nɪje]
Bulgaria	Bulharsko (n)	[bulgarsko]
Hungary	Maďarsko (n)	[madʲarsko]
Latvia	Lotyšsko (n)	[lotɪʃsko]
Lithuania	Litva (f)	[litva]
Poland	Polsko (n)	[polsko]

Romania	Rumunsko (n)	[rumunsko]
Serbia	Srbsko (n)	[srbsko]
Slovakia	Slovensko (n)	[slovɛnsko]

Croatia	Chorvatsko (n)	[horvatsko]
The Czech Republic	Česko (n)	[tʃesko]
Estonia	Estonsko (n)	[ɛstonsko]

Bosnia-Herzegovina	Bosna a Hercegovina (f)	[bosna a gɛrtsɛgowina]
Macedonia	Makedonie (f)	[makɛdoniɛ]
Slovenia	Slovinsko (n)	[slowinsko]
Montenegro	Černá Hora (f)	[tʃerna: gora]

149. Former USSR countries

| Azerbaijan | Ázerbájdžán (m) | [a:zɛrba:jdʒa:n] |
| Armenia | Arménie (f) | [armɛ:nije] |

Belarus	Bělorusko (n)	[bʰelorusko]
Georgia	Gruzie (f)	[gruzije]
Kazakhstan	Kazachstán (m)	[kazaɦsta:n]
Kirghizia	Kyrgyzstán (m)	[kɪrgɪsta:n]
Moldavia	Moldavsko (n)	[moldavsko]

| Russia | Rusko (n) | [rusko] |
| Ukraine | Ukrajina (f) | [ukrajɪna] |

Tajikistan	Tádžikistán (m)	[ta:dʒikista:n]
Turkmenistan	Turkmenistán (m)	[turkmɛnɪsta:n]
Uzbekistan	Uzbekistán (m)	[uzbɛkista:n]

150. Asia

Asia	Asie (f)	[azije]
Vietnam	Vietnam (m)	[vʰetnam]
India	Indie (f)	[indɪje]
Israel	Izrael (m)	[izraɛl]

China	Čína (f)	[tʃi:na]
Lebanon	Libanon (m)	[libanon]
Mongolia	Mongolsko (n)	[moŋolsko]

| Malaysia | Malajsie (f) | [malajzije] |
| Pakistan | Pákistán (m) | [pa:kista:n] |

Saudi Arabia	Saúdská Arábie (f)	[sau:dska: ara:bije]
Thailand	Thajsko (n)	[tajsko]
Taiwan	Tchaj-wan (m)	[tajvan]

Turkey	Turecko (n)	[turɛtsko]
Japan	Japonsko (n)	[japonsko]
Afghanistan	Afghánistán (m)	[afga:nɪsta:n]

Bangladesh	Bangladéš (m)	[baŋladɛ:ʃ]
Indonesia	Indonésie (f)	[indonɛ:zije]
Jordan	Jordánsko (n)	[jorda:nsko]

Iraq	Irák (m)	[ira:k]
Iran	Írán (m)	[i:ra:n]
Cambodia	Kambodža (f)	[kambodʒa]
Kuwait	Kuvajt (m)	[kuvajt]

Laos	Laos (m)	[laos]
Myanmar	Barma (f)	[barma]
Nepal	Nepál (m)	[nɛpa:l]
United Arab Emirates	Spojené arabské emiráty (m pl)	[spojenɛ: arabskɛ: ɛmira:tɪ]

| Syria | Sýrie (f) | [si:riɛ] |
| Palestine | Palestinská autonomie (f) | [palɛstɪnska: autonomiɛ] |

| South Korea | Jižní Korea (f) | [jɪʒni: korɛa] |
| North Korea | Severní Korea (f) | [sewerni: korɛa] |

151. North America

United States of America	Spojené státy (m pl) americké	[spojenɛ: sta:tɪ amɛriʈskɛ:]
Canada	Kanada (f)	[kanada]
Mexico	Mexiko (n)	[mɛksiko]

152. Central and South America

Argentina	Argentina (f)	[argɛntɪna]
Brazil	Brazílie (f)	[brazi:lije]
Colombia	Kolumbie (f)	[kolumbije]

| Cuba | Kuba (f) | [kuba] |
| Chile | Chile (n) | [ʧilɛ] |

| Bolivia | Bolívie (f) | [boli:wiɛ] |
| Venezuela | Venezuela (f) | [vɛnɛzuɛla] |

| Paraguay | Paraguay (f) | [paragvaj] |
| Peru | Peru (n) | [pɛru] |

Suriname	Surinam (m)	[surinam]
Uruguay	Uruguay (f)	[urugvaj]
Ecuador	Ekvádor (m)	[ɛkva:dor]

| The Bahamas | Bahamy (f pl) | [bagamɪ] |
| Haiti | Haiti (n) | [gajtɪ] |

Dominican Republic	Dominikánská republika (f)	[dominɪka:nska: rɛpublika]
Panama	Panama (f)	[panama]
Jamaica	Jamajka (f)	[jamajka]

153. Africa

Egypt	Egypt (m)	[ɛgipt]
Morocco	Maroko (n)	[maroko]
Tunisia	Tunisko (n)	[tunɪsko]

Ghana	Ghana (f)	[gana]
Zanzibar	Zanzibar (m)	[zanzibar]
Kenya	Keňa (f)	[kɛɲa]
Libya	Libye (f)	[libɪje]
Madagascar	Madagaskar (m)	[madagaskar]

Namibia	Namibie (f)	[namibiɛ]
Senegal	Senegal (m)	[sɛnɛgal]
Tanzania	Tanzanie (f)	[tanzanɪje]
South Africa	Jihoafrická republika (f)	[jɪgoafrɪtska: rɛpublika]

154. Australia. Oceania

| Australia | Austrálie (f) | [austra:lije] |
| New Zealand | Nový Zéland (m) | [novɪ: zɛ:land] |

| Tasmania | Tasmánie (f) | [tasma:nije] |
| French Polynesia | Francouzská Polynésie (f) | [frantsouska: polinɛ:zije] |

155. Cities

Amsterdam	Amsterodam (m)	[amstɛrodam]
Ankara	Ankara (f)	[aŋkara]
Athens	Atény (f pl)	[atɛ:nɪ]
Baghdad	Bagdád (m)	[bagda:d]
Bangkok	Bangkok (m)	[baŋkok]
Barcelona	Barcelona (f)	[barsɛlona]

Beijing	Peking (m)	[pɛkiŋ]
Beirut	Bejrút (m)	[bɛjru:t]
Berlin	Berlín (m)	[bɛrli:n]
Bombay, Mumbai	Bombaj (f)	[bombaj]
Bonn	Bonn (m)	[bon]

Bordeaux	Bordeaux (n)	[bordo:]
Bratislava	Bratislava (f)	[bratislava]
Brussels	Brusel (m)	[brusɛl]
Bucharest	Bukurešť (f)	[bukurɛʃtʲ]
Budapest	Budapešť (f)	[budapɛʃtʲ]

Cairo	Káhira (f)	[ka:gira]
Calcutta	Kalkata (f)	[kalkata]
Chicago	Chicago (n)	[tʃika:go]
Copenhagen	Kodaň (f)	[kodaɲ]
Dar-es-Salaam	Dar es Salaam (m)	[dar ɛs sala:m]

Delhi	Dillí (n)	[dɪli:]
Dubai	Dubaj (m)	[dubaj]
Dublin	Dublin (m)	[dublin]
Düsseldorf	Düsseldorf (m)	[dɪsldorf]

Florence	Florencie (f)	[florɛnʦije]
Frankfurt	Frankfurt (m)	[fraŋkfurt]
Geneva	Ženeva (f)	[ʒenɛva]

The Hague	Haag (m)	[ga:g]
Hamburg	Hamburk (m)	[gamburk]
Hanoi	Hanoj (m)	[ganoj]
Havana	Havana (f)	[gavana]
Helsinki	Helsinky (f pl)	[gɛlsiŋkɪ]
Hiroshima	Hirošima (f)	[giroʃima]
Hong Kong	Hongkong (m)	[goŋkoŋ]

Istanbul	Istanbul (m)	[istanbul]
Jerusalem	Jeruzalém (m)	[jeruzalɛ:m]
Kiev	Kyjev (m)	[kɪjev]
Kuala Lumpur	Kuala Lumpur (m)	[kuala lumpur]
Lisbon	Lisabon (m)	[lisabon]
London	Londýn (m)	[londɪ:n]
Los Angeles	Los Angeles (n)	[los ɛnʒɛlis]
Lyons	Lyon (m)	[lijon]

Madrid	Madrid (m)	[madrid]
Marseille	Marseille (f)	[marsɛj]
Mexico City	Mexiko (n)	[mɛksiko]
Miami	Miami (n)	[majami]
Montréal	Montreal (m)	[monrɛal]
Moscow	Moskva (f)	[moskva]
Munich	Mnichov (m)	[mniɦov]

Nairobi	Nairobi (n)	[najrobi]
Naples	Neapol (m)	[nɛapol]
New York	New York (m)	[ny: jork]
Nice	Nizza (f)	[nɪʦa]
Oslo	Oslo (n)	[oslo]
Ottawa	Otava (f)	[otava]

Paris	Paříž (f)	[parʒi:ʒ]
Prague	Praha (f)	[praga]
Rio de Janeiro	Rio de Janeiro (n)	[riodeʒanɛ:ro]
Rome	Řím (m)	[rʒi:m]

Saint Petersburg	Sankt-Petěrburg (m)	[saŋktpɛterburg]
Seoul	Soul (m)	[soul]
Shanghai	Šanghaj (f)	[ʃanɦaj]
Singapore	Singapur (m)	[siŋapur]
Stockholm	Stockholm (m)	[stokgolm]
Sydney	Sydney (n)	[sidnɛj]

Taipei	Tchaj-pej (n)	[tajpɛj]
Tokyo	Tokio (n)	[tokijo]
Toronto	Toronto (n)	[toronto]

Venice	Benátky (f pl)	[bɛnaːtkɪ]
Vienna	Vídeň (f)	[wiːdɛɲ]
Warsaw	Varšava (f)	[varʃava]
Washington	Washington (m)	[voʃiŋkton]

Printed in Great Britain
by Amazon